OPERATION SURVIVAL

—

OPERATION SURVIVAL

A Celebration of People and Nature in Scotland

From the highly acclaimed BBC Scotland television series

SALLY-ANN WILSON

Foreword by Magnus Magnusson, KBE

Supported by

THE POST OFFICE

First published in Great Britain in 1996 by
MAINSTREAM PUBLISHING COMPANY (EDINBURGH) LTD
7 Albany Street
Edinburgh EH1 3UG

ISBN 1 85158 883 3

A catalogue record for this book is available from the British Library

Typeset in Garamond
Printed and bound in Great Britain by Cambridge University Press, Cambridge

CONTENTS

Members of the Operation Survival Team

Sally-Ann Wilson, series producer

Martin Singleton, cameraman

Jane Watson, producer

Mark Smith, cameraman

Chris Watson, sound recordist

PREFACE

As we rapidly approach the start of a new millennium, I believe most people would generally agree that for all of us the environment of Scotland and the successful management of the web of relationships which bind people, economics and the natural world together is of fundamental importance if we are to preserve and perhaps, even, enhance the quality and richness of our natural heritage for future generations to enjoy.

Operation Survival has been an enthralling BBC Scotland television series. This book provides a handsome record of it as well as the opportunity to review at leisure the natural delights of Scotland and to ponder the challenges and tensions created by the needs of people, animals and plants.

As the Rio Summit in 1992 reminded us, biodiversity is good for our planet. The debate is on-going about how we – especially in our glorious rural and remote spaces – co-exist with and access our partners in biodiversity, from the Scottish Primrose to the sea eagle. This book rightly neither offers nor suggests definitive solutions; but Sally-Ann Wilson has provided us with a series of snap-shots and insights into things as diverse as the world of bats and Corncrakes, Kentish Glory Moths and Red Deer and their relationships with owners and users of their habitats. Debate is always better by being well informed.

Throughout Scotland The Post Office continues to serve communities from City centre to remotest Highland and Island. This ubiquity provides the rationale for supporting this book which with sensitivity and intelligence reminds us that survival of the diversity of our natural world in Scotland involves us all, now and always.

KENNETH GRAHAM
Chairman, Scottish Post Office Board

FOREWORD

No one who watched the BBC Scotland *Operation Survival* series could fail to be moved by the inspirational images of Scotland's diverse wildlife. In this book the series producer, Sally Wilson, has captured the emotions of the ordinary people whose lives have been touched by the wildlife which is part of their community.

Scottish Natural Heritage is delighted to have been involved in the production of both the original series and the book. They capture so well much of what SNH's work is about – the enduring partnership between people and nature.

Ranging in scale from magnificent Caledonian pinewoods and awesome sea eagles to exquisite butterflies and moths and delicate plants, the programmes illustrated the rich variety of habitats and species which make Scotland so special.

In this book of the series, Sally-Ann Wilson offers us a fascinating insight into the not-so-glamorous realities of the 'glamorous' world of the wildlife film-maker. She also introduces us to some of the interesting and dedicated people, both expert and amateur, whose work helps to ensure the survival of so many species.

Finally, I should like to give credit to partnership of a different, but equally significant, kind – the collaboration between sponsor and publisher – and thank both The Post Office and the publisher, Mainstream, without whom this book could not have been created.

MAGNUS MAGNUSSON, KBE
Chairman, Scottish Natural Heritage

INTRODUCTION

In the last 30 years the secret lives of many of the world's wild animals have been delivered to our living rooms via the small screen. Natural history films are amongst the most popular of television programmes – this is not altogether surprising since sex and survival on the African plains makes dramatic viewing.

Television has given millions of viewers a chance to become familiar with the Armadillo and the Aardvark from the comfort of their armchairs. But this fascination with exotic creatures often deflects our curiosity from the great variety of wildlife that exists on the doorstep. The people of Scotland are particularly privileged in this respect for the country is a haven for a diverse range of animals. Some of Britain's rarest species occur in Scotland and many people live their lives alongside wildlife that is rarely seen elsewhere.

The strong link between man and nature in Scotland has a long history. That this special relationship has continued to thrive is even more remarkable. It remains fundamental to the survival of our wildlife heritage and, many would argue, to the well being of the people of Scotland. Wildlife here does not exist in a vacuum. Scotland is not the UK's largest 'Nature Reserve' It is a country where the natural world is generally accepted as an integral part of daily life.

Until recently films about nature appeared to fall into two distinct categories. The majority used fabulous wildlife sequences to document the wonders of animal behaviour and biology. People were firmly excluded. The inclusion of humans it seemed would spoil the beauty of the natural world. At the opposite end of the spectrum there were those environmental programmes which highlighted just how much of the natural world has been spoilt by the human race. Such films usefully exposed the problems facing a fragile earth but their prophecies of doom and gloom were often dull and rather than worthy. These programmes rarely included the breathtaking scenes of the wild world that would inspire people to conserve.

For a film-maker, the wildlife of Scotland provided a rare opportunity: the chance to produce natural history films that included the positive role played by humans in conservation. Here, at last, was a chance to make programmes about people and wildlife living in harmony and so *Operation Survival* was conceived. The series aimed to reveal the magic of Scotland's wild places; to illustrate that special relationship between fishermen and farmers, scientists and amateur observers and the wildlife that they continue to encounter on a daily basis.

CHAPTER ONE

LOCAL HEROES

Dolphins never fail to fascinate but, like all ocean dwellers, they can be remarkably difficult to study. Although they were often the central subject of ancient tales and myths, until recently very little was known about these animals because they spend so much of their time underwater, well away from the scrutiny of researchers, scientists and casual observers.

Many species of dolphin are truly oceanic creatures, only venturing into inshore waters occasionally to breed or feed, but in the waters of the Moray Firth in north-east Scotland Bottlenose Dolphins have long been a common sight. Hugh Sutherland, now blind and in his fifties, grew up in the village of Avoch on the shores of the Firth and remembers watching the dolphins as a boy.

> I remember when I used to see them off the harbour in Avoch . . . a long time ago. I don't think they were quite as common as they are now, there were more porpoises. Of course, there were a lot more fishing-boats in the Firth in those days, too. Sometimes you could see a hundred fishing-boats out there.

Bottlenose Dolphins are found in warm oceans throughout the world. They are more bulky in shape than the Common Dolphins that also occasionally venture into the Moray Firth. In his book, *Whales of the World* (1981), Lyall Watson describes them as 'robust' animals. However, when a Moray Firth dolphin speeds out of the water for a spectacular leap just a few metres away from your boat, 'robust' seems to be rather an inadequate description. The Moray Firth is home to some of the largest Bottlenose Dolphins in the world: their blubber is extra thick, perhaps to protect them against the cold waters of the North Sea and the males can grow up to four metres in length. Harbour Porpoises are also seen regularly in the Moray Firth, usually swimming alone with their small, blunt fins just breaching the surface. Smaller and

The Dolphin Research Boat
Tursiops

more solitary than the Bottlenose Dolphin, the Harbour Porpoise is a close cousin, but belongs to a different branch of the whale family. White-beaked Dolphins, Atlantic White-sided Dolphins and Risso's Dolphins are sometimes spotted in the outer Firth but these animals rarely swim into the more confined waters where the Firth narrows.

Although frequently seen in deep ocean waters, some Bottlenose Dolphins appear to prefer shallow coastal areas. A number of animals congregate in Cardigan Bay in Wales and another resident group has recently been identified off north-west Scotland, but the best known British group are those animals that live within the large inlet of the North Sea known as the Moray Firth. From a quick glance at a map of the country it appears as though a sizable triangular nick has been taken out of the corner of the land, allowing the North Sea waters to come flooding in. Three smaller 'inner' firths – the Dornoch, Cromarty and Beauly – extend from the wider Moray Firth like long fingers of sea reaching far inland. The firths are edged with a variety of cliffs, mud flats, sands and rocky shores; all providing refuge for many species of plants and animals.

The fact that the Bottlenose Dolphins are actually resident here all year round has provided scientists with a unique opportunity to learn more about these amazing animals. It also gave the Operation Survival team a chance to document a year in the lives of some of Scotland's elusive yet most fascinating wild inhabitants.

Seals have long been the subject of controversy and scientific interest in traditional fishing areas and in 1987 Dr Paul Thompson, a zoologist from the University of Aberdeen, was awarded a grant from the Scottish Office to investigate the habits of Common and Grey Seals in the Moray Firth. As he studied the seals Paul soon realised that, although dolphins had a reputation of being notoriously difficult to watch, he was seeing Bottlenose Dolphins on a regular basis when he was out in the field. His observations were the beginnings of a long-term research project on the Bottlenose Dolphins of the Moray Firth.

The old lighthouse at Cromarty is no longer occupied by the keeper of the light but the building still has a strong link with the town's marine heritage as it has become a fitting base for the dolphin research team. The main aim of the scientists' work has been to identify the animals which spend time within the Firth. The first challenge of the project was how to find a way of being able to identify individual dolphins.

Dr Ben Wilson was the first researcher to join the team and gained his doctoral thesis by studying the dolphins' ecology. On a brilliant summer's day the *Operation Survival* team joined Ben and his colleague, Sarah Curran, on their tiny boat the *Tursiops* (Latin for 'Bottlenose dolphin') for a photographic mission. Fuel and other operating costs mean that the number of days the researchers can actually afford to spend photographing and recording the dolphins in the Firth are limited. A day such as this, with clear skies and still water, seemed a heaven-sent opportunity for both the researchers and the film crew.

As a wildlife film-maker, I have been fortunate enough to spend a great deal of time in remote and beautiful places, but I still suffer from bouts of childlike enthusiasm when a new opportunity to enjoy the natural world presents itself. The prospect of spending an entire day looking for dolphins in the company of such knowledgeable people was thrilling. We were also going to be on a tiny boat in the sun . . . I suffered my usual feelings of excited 'pre-school-outing sickness' before struggling into a mansize rubber survival suit. The clammy, oversized suit did little to dampen my enthusiasm. I know they are essential but they're not ideal wear for the hottest day of summer.

Tursiops was launched from a tiny jetty behind the Lighthouse Field Station at Cromarty with the help of an ancient Massey Ferguson tractor – it seemed to be a model which had been constructed before the company had perfected brakes! Ben obviously needed his survival suit as much for driving that tractor as for being in a boat. After getting *Tursiops* into the water, and just about keeping the tractor out of it, our planned route was to take us out of the Cromarty Firth, between the guardian hills known as 'the Sutors' and into the wider Moray Firth. From here we would steer a midline up the Firth towards Chanonry Point. In most places the Firth slopes gently away from the shore but the central channel is 40 metres deep. Once through the narrow channel between Chanonry and Fort George on the south side of the Firth, we would head for Inverness, the capital town of the Highlands with a population of some

Counting Dolphins: Hugh Sutherland with guide dog Matthew

13

40,000 people. At Inverness we would pass under the impressive span of the Kessock Bridge before turning in to land at Kessock pier.

Only one part of a Bottlenose Dolphin is regularly visible in the wild – its sickle-shaped dorsal fin. By taking close-up photographs of numerous fins the research team have built up a gallery of dolphin fin, rather than mug, shots. As the pictures were gathered it quickly became clear that dolphin fins are very different and each has its own individual characteristics and markings. Dorsal fins vary in size and shape, some are pointed, others more rounded at the tip, some appear to grow almost vertically from the animal's back, like the fin of a Killer Whale, while others are swept back. Many dolphins have nicks and notches in their fins from fights and most have distinctive coloured markings on the skin, blotches and patches of a lighter hue.

We had only just passed between the Sutors and out into the Moray Firth itself when Sarah spotted a group of dolphins. Her camera clicked quickly into action as she attempted to add to the project's portrait gallery of fins.

> Oh, fantastic! They're swimming right in front of the boat. That's number 116. See, he's got a white fringe to the fin and then a nick just on the trailing edge. We've not seen him here since February. It's wonderful to be able to get to know individuals – they all seem to have different characters – and to be able to follow a calf until it's three or four years old and begins to make its own way in the world.

The water of the Firth was still and petrol-blue. Two groups of dolphins, apparently mothers with calves, swam alongside us only occasionally breaking the surface to take breath. Seeing an animal with a calf is one of the easiest ways to prove the sex of an individual dolphin in the field. Calves remain with their mothers for up to four years, gradually exploring further and further afield, so any animal with a youngster is almost certain to be a female. Young dolphins are quite distinctive, they are just under a metre long at birth and much paler than the adults. Following the birth the mother will often push the youngster to the surface for its first breath. If she is too weakened by labour to do this, other female dolphins will give the calf the necessary shove. This is just one example of the co-operation that seems to exist among the female dolphins as they raise their young. In one group that we watched the adults swam on the outside protecting the two calves between them. Sarah has noticed that on occasions other dolphins in the group will 'baby-sit', giving the mothers a chance to forage further afield. Males rarely form part of these groups for any length of time, apparently they just visit the group to court and mate with the females.

Ben described the Moray Firth dolphins as living in a 'fission and fusion society'. It sounded fun! In fact, this means that the dolphins don't live in distinct family groups as we would perhaps like to imagine but frequently move between one group and another. In other parts of the world young males usually swim in twos and threes but in the Firth they

Dolphins never fail to fascinate . . .

Dr Ben Wilson and Sarah Curran compare slides to identify individual dolphins

are often seen swimming alone. Ben thinks that this may be because there isn't the same risk of shark attacks in the colder waters of north-east Scotland.

Everything that Ben and Sarah explained about dolphin behaviour seemed to be illustrated by what we saw; the day was turning into the ultimate interactive zoology lesson. As I was sitting in the bow a young male swam up to the boat. He crisscrossed in front of us, hitching a ride from the push of the pressure wave created as the boat forced its way through the water. He seemed to squeak with excitement every time he shot out of the water, although for those few precious moments I am sure the excitement was all mine. His skin was taught and shiny but his back was covered with deep white scars and his dorsal fin looked like the battered ears of an elderly tom cat. Ben laughed and said that he was named Tamieiso, short for This is A Male If Ever I Saw One! As Sarah had pointed out, the dolphins seem to have distinctive characters and this one had the reputation of being rather a rough lad. His scars and wounds were attributed to his adolescent scraps with other dolphins.

Ben steered a straight course and maintained a steady speed. The dolphins would join us if they were interested in our company but we wouldn't be harassing them. Soon another group of dolphins came alongside us; Ben's tactic had paid off.

> Yes, yes, yes! We're coming up to them now and you can see them underwater, they're being really co-operative just letting us come alongside. They're probably foraging along here in the kelpy, rocky bottom. They dive down for about two minutes, although they can stay down for five. When the sun's like this you can really see the skin marks and lesions. It's a bit worrying – marks like this are really unusual on Bottlenose Dolphins. In Florida, California, or wherever, the same dolphins don't have these kind of marks. Here 90 per cent of the dolphins seem to be marked. See, that calf's covered, it's got black blotches all over its skin. It's really unusual . . . I wonder what it is.?

Once the research team started to identify animals on a regular basis the dolphins could be counted and their movements monitored. The picture that emerged of dolphin life and behaviour in the Firth was a fascinating one, far more complex than anyone could have predicted and the stories of the dolphins' lives have become like a soap opera unfolding in the waters of the Firth. The scientists here have presented the results of their research to scientific audiences around the world; the fin photographs have even been circulated to other British and European dolphin study groups to form a sort of 'Dolphin Interpol'. As Ben explained, the team has made a lot of progress since the project began.

> Four years ago I was optimistic, until I went to sea. When I started the research it was so confusing, dolphins were all over the place and how on earth were we going to get an idea

of their social structure and what they were doing? But just by doing surveys over and over again we began to build up patterns. It's been very rewarding to see how they are interacting and pick up clues about what they do and why they're here.

Bottlenose Dolphin leaping in front of Kessock Bridge, Inverness

The real joy of these dolphins is that they are also easily seen from the land. The dolphins regularly swim close to the shore, particularly where the Firth is narrowed by the long spit of land known as Chanonry Point. It's on this point that Hugh Sutherland now spends his summer evenings, along with his guide dog, Matthew, and a group of voluntary dolphin watchers. The beach at Chanonry provides a superb view of the water on both sides of the point and from here the group carefully records the time and details of any dolphin sightings. Although he can no longer see the dolphins, Hugh can often hear them breathing when they swim close to the beach and by listening to the time on a recorded clock as he sits by the shore, he calls out the exact time of the dolphins' arrival to the rest of the team.

A number of groups of voluntary watchers have been formed. Some, like the Friends of the Moray Firth Dolphins which is based in Findochty, are formally organised, others are more casual observers who take notes and keep in touch with the Cromarty Lighthouse research team. To produce successful results a project such as this requires a great deal of long-term inquiry and research. As Ben acknowledged, the research team can't be out in the Firth all the time and so far the observations of other

Only one part of a Dolphin is regularly visible – its sickle-shaped dorsal fin

people have provided the team with some very useful information about dolphin behaviour and distribution.

Because of their high profile the Bottlenose Dolphins of the Moray Firth seem to have become a sort of totem animal adopted by many of the towns and villages around the Firth. In summer there are dolphins everywhere – plastic dolphins, rubber dolphins, porcelain dolphins, flower dolphins – the Firth has become the centre of a dolphin industry. The universal appeal of dolphins has great commercial value for local communities and their image adorns many shop fronts, from the Dolphin Café nestling beneath the Kessock Bridge at Inverness to a rather unlikely logo advertising a specialist roller-blind shop. Paul Thompson sees the way that the dolphins have focused attention on the marine environment as a good thing.

> In an area like the Moray Firth where so many people live on the coast it's quite clear that these people and their associated industries are changing the dolphins' environment. Our research is trying to pre-empt the problems that inevitably rise from all of that. The dolphins are providing a focus, highlighting problems not only for them but also for us. Hopefully, that focus will be used to protect the habitat and not just as another way of exploiting creatures like the dolphins.

18

The dolphins have definitely become a community symbol but, after an exhilarating ten hours in the *Tursiops*, it was the Dolphin Café symbol that seemed most appealing to film crew and dolphin researchers alike. Tea and chips on dry land gave us plenty of opportunity to consider the results of a very special day. As we had rounded Chanonry Point we had been treated to a dolphin's-eye view of the colourful assortment of humans who lined the beach – children squeaking with sounds of excitement not unlike the squeals of the dolphins; adults with eyes glued to telescopes and cameras waiting for the next dolphin to leap. Behind us a single dolphin, identified as number 19, spun into the air in front of a fishing-boat *en route* to Inverness.

Once past Chanonry, the weather changed and the sea became less calm. It was no longer easy to spot the dolphins from their 'footprints' (smooth marks in the still water where they had recently broken the surface for a breath). Instead, we were constantly mistaking wave crests for dolphin fins whilst trying to hold all the electrical and technical paraphernalia of filming in place against the swell of the water. For the final stage of our journey I drew the producer's short straw . . . the crew stayed out in the very fresh air while I wedged my outsized rubber-clad body in *Tursiops'* tiny cabin with the monitors, camera, leads and a lot of petrol fumes. I consoled myself with an emergency packet of chocolate raisins and the thought that in one day we had probably seen a quarter of the 130 Bottlenose Dolphins that live in the Moray Firth.

The children of North Kessock Primary School look out at the Firth from their playground and most of them see the dolphins on a regular basis. It's a privilege denied to many young people in the country and the children of North Kessock are well aware of their special relationship with the sea and its creatures.

> I like to see them playing in the water because they jump in all different directions; they're usually quite near the shore. I always go to my gran's and watch them. I'd be bored if they weren't there.

> Dolphins are nice; it would be a shame to see them go away so, if we help them, they'll help us. They probably do more for us than we do for them.

> People like us aren't helping the dolphins because we use cans with aerosols that go up into the ozone layer and that affects the sunlight which affects the whole food chain as well.

Scotland is not a large country but most of its people live in the so called 'central belt', the narrow neck of the country close to the English border, with Edinburgh on the east coast and Glasgow on the west. This concentration of people in a few urban areas means that vast tracts of the countryside remain uninhabited and for those that live in the towns and

Bottlenose Dolphins and oil rigs in the Cromarty Firth

cities its not always easy to see and enjoy the natural world.

Julie Oswald has grown up on Glasgow's Castlemilk estate. She lives less than an hour's journey from unspoilt countryside but, like many other teenagers in urban areas, Julie has had few opportunities to explore the wild places that exist on her doorstep. She is fascinated by whales and dolphins, her room is covered in posters of these magnificent animals as they breach and twist out of the water in foreign sunsets. It's an interest that Julie shares with her mother, June, but neither have ever seen a wild dolphin. They have, however, joined the Whale and Dolphin Conservation Society and adopted one of the Moray Firth dolphins through the society's 'Adopt a Dolphin' scheme. As part of the *Operation Survival* programme Julie, June and Julie's younger brother, Richard, travelled to Inverness to try and see their dolphin.

Most people who live around the Firth are well aware of the benefits that the dolphins bring to the area and of the need to conserve them and their environment. Bill Fraser owns 'Dolphin Ecosse', a company that operates boat tours from Cromarty. The animals have given Bill a chance to establish a successful business in his native town, following a career in the Navy. Like the three other approved operators in the area, Bill is well aware of the need for care when taking people to see the dolphins. Pressure from too many boat trips could pose a threat to the animals, but no dolphins means no business, so there is a clear incentive for operators to stick to a code of practice that ensures the dolphins will not be harmed. The Oswalds have adopted Sundance, a young male dolphin with a distinctive spot on his fin. The family joined one of the regular dolphin-watching boat trips that operate from Cromarty harbour. There's plenty of information on board about the animals and identification cards explain Sundance's own family history. After an hour on the boat, a small group of dolphins appear alongside. The dolphins usually swim in groups of females and calves or parties of three or four young males; on occasions 20 or 30 of the Firth's 130 dolphins can be seen together.

Sundance was born in 1990 and is the son of Splash, one of the senior females in the Moray Firth dolphin group. At four years old he no longer swims with his mother, who has a new calf. Instead, Sundance is usually to be found with two other young males in a group affectionately known by the researchers as 'The Three Amigos'. Sadly, Sundance wasn't among the dolphins that the Oswald family followed but seeing the animals in the wild certainly made a forceful impression on Julie.

> I feel a part of it and it's part of our country. I think it's sad that Glasgow schoolchildren never get out here. We take them to zoos and show them animals that aren't even native to this country. We should bring them up here and show them what conservation's all about. Show them these animals that are wild and that have their freedom but also tell them about the threat to their survival and the part that they can play in helping in their conservation.

Bottlenose Dolphins use sound rather than sight to hunt for fish. Visibility in the Firth is limited, not by pollution but because of natural disturbance and debris in the turbulent waters – even if the dolphins possessed superb eyesight, it would be of little use for fishing in the Firth. Instead, the dolphins rely on their highly sophisticated 'echo location' sound system for hunting. Echo location enables the dolphins to form a clear impression of their surroundings without actually being able to see what is around them in the water. They produce 'clicks' in hollow spaces inside their skulls and direct these clicks at objects, rather as we would shine the beam of a torch to pick out items in the dark. A rapid interpretation of the echo they receive back from the clicks gives them plenty of detail about the object – whether or not it is a potential meal (such as Herring or Salmon), its size, speed and direction of travel.

For the *Operation Survival* team underwater filming of the Moray Firth dolphins also proved tricky because of the poor visibility. Many days were spent on a variety of boats with small video cameras strapped, often precariously, on to booms over the side of the craft. Sometimes we saw dolphins, sometimes we didn't. At first even if the animals were seen they were rarely filmed. It's one of the hard lessons of natural history film-making: people will, if charmed, bribed, cosseted and coaxed, usually agree to appear in the film and take direction. Wild animals? Well, they just don't take orders. Even Stephen Spielberg would be hard pressed to get wild dolphins to co-operate.

Although we were rarely able to film the dolphins underwater, Chris Watson, the team's specialist wildlife sound recordist, took the opportunity of being out in the boat to make plenty of recordings. These revealed to us a new but crucial dimension of the dolphins' world. With Chris's hydrophones (special underwater microphones), we could hear the dolphins' echo-locating clicks as they steered their way through the murky waters. If they were close by, we could even hear them breathing. We listened in to the other wildlife of the Firth: a roar like that of a lion belonged to a male Common Seal. It was a wonderful opportunity to build a fresh picture of the marine life of the Moray Firth. But obscuring it all, crashing in from every quarter with bangs and creaks, thumps and whirs, were the sounds of a non-natural world; the sounds of human disturbance.

Chris is very particular, obsessional in fact, about 'sound'. A tall, rather imposing man, he reserves what can only be described as a particularly withering look for producers and directors who dare to ask him to record 'noises' to accompany the pictures. 'Noise,' he correctly points out, is 'a harsh, disagreeable sound . . . a din', whereas sounds are a 'mental impression created by something we have heard'. After a recording session in the Firth, just for once even Chris agreed that he had recorded 'noise', and lots of it. Sound waves travel four times more efficiently through water than through air and on occasions it seemed that we could hear every boat and motor in the entire Firth. Engines spluttered and thumped, chains rattled. Putting on the headphones and listening to the sounds picked up by the hydrophone revealed a horrible, discordant and jarring underwater environment. But it is the dolphins' environment, they have no option but to live in it.

The Firth has been a busy shipping route for many hundreds of years. From historic accounts, as well as the memories of older residents such as Hugh Sutherland, it is also clear that dolphins have been present here for a long time. It can quite rightly be argued that the dolphins have chosen to remain in the area despite the presence of fishing-boats and cargo ships. But, then again, shipping used to be much less 'noisy', sail only giving way to motor in the last 150 years. And the herring fleets and coal boats headed for Inverness would not have chased the dolphins. No doubt some mariners would have noted the animals out of curiosity but it is only in recent years that people have been inquisitive enough about the dolphins to actually try and follow them for any length of time.

Bottlenose Dolphins are protected by both British and European laws that make it an offence to 'deliberately disturb' any species of whale or dolphin. But these are highly mobile animals, living in 5,300 square kilometres of water, and it may be difficult to prove whether any disturbance has been caused by 'deliberate' action.

Holly Arnold has been working with the researchers at Cromarty Lighthouse, the Scottish Wildlife Trust, Scottish Natural Heritage and the EU Life Programme to develop a code of practice for all boat users within the Firth. Under the code of conduct known as 'The Dolphin Space Programme', operators are expected to stick to an agreed route, keep a steady speed and slow down gradually on sighting dolphins. Operators who have been accredited by the programme have also agreed to limit their visits to high-pressure areas, such as the Kessock Channel and Chanonry Narrows, and to avoid marine pollution and physical contact with the animals.

Dolphins are sociable animals and they also use sound to communicate with each other. Each animal has its own distinctive 'signature' whistle, allowing other dolphins within the group to identify it. Dolphin language is also composed of whines, groans and jaw clapping. As yet, many of the sounds have not been translated by humans, although the proximity of researchers to the Moray Firth animals obviously provides excellent research opportunities.

Vincent Janik is a German scientist based at St Andrews University in Fife. As an expert on the sounds of the marine world, Vincent has become a vital contributor to the dolphin research project. Our wildlife sound recordist, Chris Watson, often has conversations – long, detailed debates – about bird song but, in Vincent Janik, Chris had met his match! The two met up at Cromarty Pier early one morning to discuss microphones, hydrophones and multi-tracks. They placed a hydrophone over the end of the pier and donned headphones to eavesdrop on the underwater world. 'It was like a dawn chorus,' Chris said. Pistol Shrimps cracked and popped, then, as a bop-bopping sound like an old motorbike approached, Vincent said, 'Cod'. Just as a birdwatcher might say, 'male Hen Harrier, flying right,' Vincent pronounced, 'female Hake in front of us with Moray Eel to the left'.

Following their fishy morning recital, Chris and Vincent continued to discuss the problems of recording the dolphins. Vincent needed to be able to drop hydrophones into various positions in the Firth and then to listen to the sounds they picked up from his onshore location. If he remained in a boat to listen to the recordings his presence might influence the dolphins' behaviour and in any case the sound of the boat engine would interfere with the recording. Ideally, Vincent wanted to be able to listen in to more than one hydrophone at any one time, yet he couldn't leave a trail of sound cables crossing the busy waterway. Chris demonstrated the radio microphones, or 'radio mics' as they are known, which are used to transmit sounds to a recorder via radio waves rather than endless leads and cables. In television, radio mics are attached to a reporter's lapel or jumper, allowing them the freedom to rove around at some distance from the sound recordist without ugly leads being seen in the camera shot. Vincent was obviously impressed. Within days a curtain of hydrophones with radio mics attached were in place in the water off the Kessock Channel, the narrow part of the Firth near Inverness. Vincent could drive to a nearby point on the shore and pick up the sounds of the dolphins from the hydrophones. He recorded these on to a multi-track tape recorder and a sophisticated system of calculations enabled him not only to record the dolphins but to plot their positions in the water and their subsequent movement in relation to the row of hydrophones.

Vincent Janik was obviously fortunate in having such a rare opportunity to eavesdrop on these intriguing animals. But now curious members of

Harry Ross preparing to examine dead Harbour Porpoise

the public can also listen in to the dolphins. The hydrophones at Kessock have been linked up to the Dolphin and Seal Information Centre just over the Kessock Bridge on the A9 and also to the new Environmental Education Centre at South Kessock.

Watching, listening and recording reveal more and more about dolphin life. Kess is believed to be a female dolphin often seen in the Kessock area, which seems to be a favourite feeding ground for her. The researchers have already noticed that, while many dolphins seem to change their habits according to the season, other individuals show a clear preference for specific areas, particularly places where the Firth narrows, such as Kessock and Chanonry. Inevitably, these are the areas where the dolphins are most likely to come into conflict with human activity. Because dolphins are easily seen in these places, they have become popular with tourist boat operators, yet we already understand from Vincent Janik's work that in these narrows all sounds are amplified by the shape of the Firth. Kessock is also the part of the Firth closest to Inverness, one of the fastest growing towns in Scotland. For many years the town's sewage outfall has emptied directly into the Firth at Kessock, although there are plans to build a new sewage outfall much farther out into the sea by the end of the century.

Kess, famed for her spectacular leaps beneath the Kessock Bridge, clearly has a deformed spine – her back has a distinct and unsightly twist – and a similar deformity was also noted in one of her calves. Kess has sadly lost two of her three most recent calves and another two animals which were regularly seen in the Kessock area are also known to have died. No one is certain about the causes of these deaths but it is difficult not to conclude that the human impact on their environment has just been too great for this particular group of Moray Firth dolphins. To anyone who has never been fortunate enough to see even a single wild dolphin, a group numbering over one hundred animals must sound very large. In fact, in biological terms this is a small and, therefore, vulnerable population. It would take very little – an oil pollution incident, an increase in wildlife tourism, or a significant build-up of existing pollution and disturbance threats – to push the population of Moray Firth Bottlenose Dolphins over the edge of viability.

Inevitably, dolphins do die. The natural lifespan of a Bottlenose Dolphin may be an impressive 40 or 50 years but, like all creatures, there can be many reasons for life to be cut short. When a dead animal is washed ashore it is described as being 'stranded'. Larger whales and dolphins (those animals longer than 7.5 metres) are referred to as 'royal fish', this means that they are the property of the crown and must be reported as having been found stranded, but smaller cetaceans, like dolphins and the Harbour Porpoise, are usually only reported on a voluntary basis. Since 1992, veterinary scientist Harry Ross has been studying strandings, examining the carcasses of many different species, in the Scottish Agricultural College's Veterinary Investigations laboratory in Inverness. He has performed post mortem examinations, checking the pathology, disease and, where possible, pollution levels in each animal. He can tell the age of a dolphin by examining its teeth – dolphin teeth

Bottlenose Dolphin with calf

have growth rings similar to those seen in trees.

Operation Survival filmed Harry at work in his laboratory.

> Conservation, in its broadest sense, means that we have to
> know the whole spectrum of the animal's life and its death.
> We must understand the natural causes of death to know
> what effect man is having on the animals.

Finding out about and understanding natural causes of death certainly
makes it clear when something is triggering 'unnatural' death. More used
to analysing farm animals Harry Ross quickly became embroiled in the
quest to discover more about the sea mammals of the Firth. As the study
continued, Harry began to realise that he was involved in a complex and
fascinating natural mystery.

People like Hugh Sutherland, who have lived alongside the dolphins
for many years, have often remarked that the Harbour Porpoise once
seemed more common in the Firth. But these are unobtrusive animals,
even more difficult to study and count than dolphins. In the first two
years of his research, however, Harry noted that Harbour Porpoises were
the most commonly stranded animals in the Firth. He examined no less
than 105 dead Harbour Porpoises, 42 of which had clearly died from
what he described as 'multiple trauma injuries'.

I stood beside Harry as he examined an adult porpoise. It's always sad
to see a dead whale of any kind but I couldn't help being fascinated at the

Bottlenose Dolphins attacking a Harbour Porpoise

chance to examine the animal's superb design. Wearing latex gloves to protect me from infection, I was able to touch the taut skin with its wonderful marbled patterning. This creature was crafted to perfection, the rounded head and smooth skin enabled it to slip through the water with little resistance or drag. But as Harry turned the animal over a familiar story was revealed to him. The underside of the porpoise was raked with parallel cuts and scratches. He was sure that an internal examination of this animal, like that of others, would uncover extensive injuries – fractured ribs, perforated lungs and a ruptured liver. Harry was faced with a mammoth piece of detective work. He discussed the mystery with Ben Wilson and the team at the lighthouse.

The animals had clearly been injured as a result of a high-energy impact of some kind. They mulled over every possible cause for the injuries: damage from fishing gear, impact by boats, injury caused by seismic exploration for oil in the Firth. But none of these human activities would cause such a regular pattern of injury to porpoises. Every animal seemed to have been struck in the same place on its body. Could another marine animal have inflicted the injuries? Ben at first suspected that seals had been playing with dead porpoises, raking the bodies with their claws, but there were often six parallel scratches and seals only have five claws. Orca or Killer Whales do sometimes come into the Firth but all of the porpoise carcasses were intact. As a predatory animal, Killer Whales would have been eating at least part of the porpoise. Then the suspicion fell on the dolphins themselves.

Acquiring forensic evidence was the next step. The jaw of a Bottlenose Dolphin was held against the cuts on the porpoise. The dolphin's peg-like teeth were a perfect match for the injuries to the porpoise but the final conclusions were drawn with the help of one of the Chanonry dolphin watchers.

Mike Haycox had spent 350 hours videoing and watching the dolphins.

> When you first see them, that's the best time. It's a very emotive, almost magical experience; you get this glimpse of another world.

Mike was videoing the dolphins one day in April when he noticed something unusual in their behaviour.

> Two dolphins were throwing a Salmon or another type of fish around in the water. I filmed it but didn't really think any more about it. When I showed it to the lighthouse researchers they went wild. I'd filmed a porpoise being attacked by a dolphin which no one had ever witnessed before, let alone filmed.

For Harry Ross the video had provided the final piece of the jigsaw.

> I wasn't optimistic that we would ever be able to demonstrate this happening but I am delighted that we now have film of it actually occurring. The aggressive behaviour of the dolphins is difficult to explain: it could be territorial, it could be competition for the same food source. The possibility of dolphins making a mistake in their sonar is extremely unlikely as Bottlenose Dolphin sonar is exquisite.

Since Mike Haycox produced his video evidence two more amateur cameramen have recorded dolphins attacking Harbour Porpoise. All of these incidents were shown as part of the *Operation Survival* programme.

It had been quite a year following the dolphins and researchers, but no one had expected that such a fascinating side of the dolphins' behaviour would be revealed. The story of the Bottlenose Dolphins' aggressive behaviour made international news headlines. Ben and Harry were repeatedly asked for comments and, as the programme's producer, I was interviewed for many news stations around the world. The direction of questioning was nearly always the same: 'But these are friendly, smiling dolphins, just like the famous television dolphin, Flipper. People imbue them with magical powers of health-giving and healing. People are

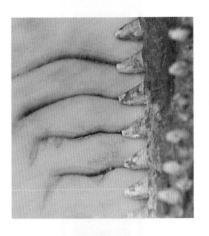

Perfect evidence. Bottlenose Dolphin teeth are matched to scars on a dead porpoise

Mike Haycox videoing dolphins from Chanonry Point

desperate to swim with them, communicate with them. Have we got it wrong? Are they really vicious and dangerous animals, some kind of natural psychopathic killers?'

As we edited the programme I had lots of time to think. I felt sure that the mysterious attacks on the porpoises had actually revealed as much about human behaviour as it had about Bottlenose Dolphins.

In a world that seems increasingly full of wars and stress, people are only too aware of the rather imperfect nature and behaviour of their own kind . . . the human animal. To alleviate our own feelings of failure as a truly social species I suspect that we have sought those ideal characteristics in other animals. Very little was known about Bottlenose Dolphins but they seemed intelligent; the mothers appeared caring and we hoped they lived in established family groups. The line of their long mouths that continued under trunk-like jaws appeared to give them a permanent smile. The reaction of shock and horror to dolphins as apparently unprovoked killers of other whales was an outlet for human disappointment. Our bitter disappointment is in recognition of the fact that the social world of the dolphin is no more perfect and rosy than our own. I have had to ask myself the question 'would the media interest in this story have been as great if the cause of so many porpoise deaths had been a human one?'

For the researchers the discovery has meant more work as they try to establish the reasons for the dolphins' behaviour. For Harry Ross it was an exciting discovery but not one that affected his love of dolphins.

> I don't think we need to change our perceptions of dolphins, they are absolutely fantastic animals, but it does underline what really is obvious – they are wild animals and wild animal behaviour can sometimes be fairly traumatic.

Researcher Sarah Curran has always believed that our interest in dolphins should be in what they are and not what we would like them to be.

> We should appreciate them for being different to us, different animals living in a different environment, and not because we think they are like us.

But it was Ben Wilson who, for me, summed up the true spirit of our fascination with the Bottlenose Dolphins of the Moray Firth.

> A lot of people see dolphins as wonderful, mythical animals but you only have to go out there to see that they're not. They're certainly very exciting and they are always up to different things and they appear to be very intelligent, but they live in a real world. We examine animals with skin lesions and we actually see them fighting with one another, causing marks to each other. We have to appreciate that these are real animals out there, living in a real world and trying to find food for themselves and their young.

A dolphin is depicted on the Shandwick stone, a Pictish symbol stone near the north shore of the Moray Firth . . . it would seem that Bottlenose Dolphins have been Local Heroes here for many hundreds of years.

Bottlenose Dolphin in front of Chanonry Lighthouse

CHAPTER TWO

THE CALL OF COLL

The Corncrake may be one of Britain's rarest breeding birds but it is not a distinctive creature . . . at least not in appearance. But the call of the male Corncrake is rather a different matter, it has been variously described as 'rasping', 'harsh', and 'discordant'. The sound of his crake is rather like that made by a young boy blowing through a paper covered comb, or the sound my grandfather produced as he sharpened blades on a grinding stone. The sort of sound that makes your teeth water. It is also loud. Very loud, which is a surprise as the male Corncrake is quite a small bird, only 30 centimetres in length from bill to tail.

In centuries past, the Corncrake bred throughout Scotland. Between April and July summer meadows everywhere used to rattle with their raucous calling. Having heard a Corncrake in full cry, it comes as no surprise that not all memories of the bird (when it was more widespread) are fond ones, for the Corncrake does like to do the bulk of his calling at night. One suspects that throughout history more than one boot or pot has been tossed in the night from a Hebridean croft door in sheer frustration at the racket produced by the birds.

Hugh Mackinnon is a 'Collach', a resident of the tiny Hebridean island of Coll which has a population of only 160 people. Now in his eighties, he still lives in a row of low whitewashed cottages in the island's village of Arinagour. As he tends his fading yellow roses, Hugh remembers the time when every one of the island's tiny fields was occupied by a Corncrake during the summer months.

> You see that field over by the war memorial? There used to be one in there and he went on all night, never a halt, and I used to say to myself, 'funny he isn't getting tired'. They're lovely creatures.

As another elderly resident of the island pointed out to Hugh, the noise created by the birds had some advantages – 'They called so loud you couldn't hear whether the girls said yes or no!'

> The call is a bit rough but I think it's wonderful. People didn't used to bother about them, the Corncrake was there and that was that. I suppose they were annoying to some people, right enough, but you got used to them. Of course, we worked hard in those days and you'd sleep anyway whether the birds were craking or not.

Nowadays the birds are mostly found on the southern tip of the island where the Royal Society for the Protection of Birds (RSPB) has a nature reserve.

> I think that when the mowing machines and reapers started cutting the fields many Corncrake eggs were destroyed by the machines running over the nests. I hope they will come back again. I'm sure that they will.

Certainly the birds do seem to be returning in greater numbers to Coll. Since the reserve was purchased in 1991 there has been a noticeable increase in the number of pairs of birds breeding there, from six to 31 (1995).

It was important that the *Operation Survival* programmes should illustrate a wide variety of habitats and species, and so portray the magnificent variety and diversity of Scotland's wildlife. If we were going to make a programme about a bird, then the Corncrake seemed an ideal choice. It nested in an unusual habitat and, from what little was known of it, it was a bird with attitude and a great deal of character. Mark Smith, the main wildlife cameraman for *Operation Survival*, saw things a little differently. Or rather, he perceived things differently; seeing was, he felt, the nub of the problem. Corncrakes have perfected the behaviour that many small children aspire to – they are easily heard but rarely seen. Even the most experienced bird watchers rarely spend time actually observing these avian fiends. How was Mark to make a film about an animal that spends its entire life trying to remain invisible?

However, Chris Watson, our sound recordist, was positively effervescent with enthusiasm. Chris saw it as an opportunity to break new ground in wildlife film-making; to him pictures are only incidental anyway . . . just think of the soundtrack he could record on Coll. Snipe drumming in marshy fields, Starlings gathering to roost and the Corncrake calling. But despite Chris's enthusiasm we weren't making a radio programme; *Operation Survival* did need pictures of the bird. News of an RSPB research project encouraged us – if scientists were going to be catching the Corncrakes then Mark stood a better chance of filming them. In February we set off on our first visit to Coll.

The Corncrake is not a permanent island resident, the birds spend the winter in southern Africa, returning to Coll to breed in April each year. Corncrakes were once a common British bird but as farming methods changed the number of birds returning to nest each year dwindled. Now the Corncrake's call is only occasionally heard in mainland Britain, but

Male Corncrake displaying

the birds do still return to Scottish islands like Coll, in the Hebrides and to Orkney. Our task on this initial visit to Coll was to set the scene and show the island's preparation for the birds' spring arrival. I think, on reflection, that we would have been more comfortable filming them in their winter quarters! Coll is supposed to be one of the windiest places in Britain and it certainly lived up to its reputation during that first trip. Hebridean islands are typically thought of as crofting communities. But while the crofting system of land tenure still endures on the neighbouring island of Tiree, the people of Coll maintain and work their own farms rather than crofts. However, farming is not the high-intensity agribusiness that it has become on the mainland. Herbicides and sprays are not widely used and the pace of life and farming are less frantic, with many tasks still undertaken by hand rather than with machinery. Cattle graze the coastal meadows, their dung mixing with wind-blown shell sand to form the rich organic soil of the machair. In spring and early summer the machair is a brilliant carpet of wildflowers, including many rare species that depend on this unusual mixture of shell and dung. The hay from the meadows is eventually cut and fed to the livestock in winter. It is also in the machair meadows that the Corncrake likes to nest. Although the Corncrakes are only summer visitors to Coll, their stay on the island depends on the traditional, year-round farming practices.

My academic explanation of how machair soils are formed did little to console a frozen Mark Smith as he sat under a waterproof sheet, filming Coll farmer Alan Brodie as he fed his livestock with machair hay at first light on a freezing February morning. The weather is an eternal problem for wildlife film-makers: it is always either too hot or too cold, too wet or, just occasionally, too dry. Regular supplies of chocolate biscuits did little to lift Mark's spirits in the driving sleet. After years of working alongside wildlife cameramen, I am convinced that they are a breed apart: some kind of 'super-human', capable of remaining crouched for hours in small, smelly and very uncomfortable places, waiting and waiting for animal action. Waiting alongside them, I've often found myself drifting off into a dream world, yet the cameraman must remain poised – the second the animals start to 'behave' the camera needs to be running. They are the unsung heroes on which our craft depends.

The next climatic challenge for Mark on Coll was to film the wind-blown shell sand. This time he spent hours huddled on the crest of the exposed dunes for a dramatic shot of the 'windiest place in Britain'. He got the shot, but the sand blasted his camera and caused unbelievable damage to his tripod.

A far more common bird, the Starling, was to have a cameo role in our Corncrake film. Much maligned and often taken for granted these birds are both colourful and characterful – just look more closely at the iridescent sheen of a Starling's feathers next time one is scrapping over the bird-table offerings. If it was a rare, tropical bird we would marvel at the purples and greens of its plumage. Starlings gather together to roost in the winter and scientists now believe that the birds exchange information about feeding sites during these communal gatherings. Each night as dusk sets in the birds swirl in small flocks, settling briefly here on a

The Castles Breachacha

telegraph wire, there on a roof ridge. Every time the birds take off their numbers swell until finally they form a twisting column of silhouettes against the sunset. Then, with great speed, the column is sucked, as if by a vacuum, into the roost site itself. On Coll one of the largest Starling roosts is in the old castle at Breachacha. This gothic style building is actually the new castle – the original castle, built in the fifteenth century, stands a few hundred yards away, has been renovated and is now inhabited once again. The Starlings' roost, on the other hand, is pure Hitchcock: thousands of birds, their wings sharply outlined against the orange sky, whirl around the castle's turrets. Soon this flock would begin to split up; as the spring days lengthened many of the birds would leave the island to nest elsewhere.

By late March there is an air of expectation on Coll. Charlie Self, the RSPB warden, tries to encourage the rough vegetation to grow by spreading cow manure along fences and in field corners. This will encourage nettles and other growth to form corridors and pockets of deep, dense cover that will appeal to the shy birds and allow them to scuttle from site to site without the need to cross open ground.

Brian and Moira MacIntyre have a farm near the RSPB reserve. One Corncrake has regularly returned to establish his territory in a corner of the field opposite their house. Moira always keeps an ear open for the bird's arrival.

> You look forward to the spring, and the Corncrake is part of
> the spring. If you hear the Corncrake you know, at least you
> hope, that the better weather is coming.

Even Brian isn't put off by the bird's highly vocal return:

> I quite enjoy the noise. If you're a heavy sleeper, it doesn't
> bother you . . . I don't find it offensive at all.

But on more than one occasion the MacIntyres have been conned.
They've rushed to the window, excited by the return of their Corncrake
. . . only to see a solitary Starling sitting on the fence. These birds are
wonderful mimics, and one of the island's resident Starlings has learnt to
copy the call of the Corncrake – and copy it very well. Chris was
delighted with his recording of a Starling performing as a Corncrake; this
was definitely one for the archives. We just hoped that within a few days
he would also record the Corncrake performing as himself.

By April it is not only the birds that return to the island. Glen Tyler,
RSPB researcher, joined Charlie with the *Operation Survival* film crew in
keen pursuit. Glen is a well-known and inventive researcher of 'difficult'
birds, always devising cunning new means to learn more about his quarry.
He has already completed a study of the Bittern, another shy bird with a
big call, but the Corncrake offered new and exciting possibilities for
discovery.

> The Corncrake is a very special bird because it's threatened
> with global extinction. It is a bird that has declined very
> quickly in the UK – within living memory it was quite
> common in many places. It's also an interesting bird in its
> own right; an unusual member of its family, it lives on land
> whereas most other rails and crakes live in wetland habitats.

Once the birds have returned, Glen's first aim is to catch the males and
attach tiny radio transmitters to their tail feathers. Each transmitter emits
a slightly different signal allowing Glen to follow and identify individual
birds. But before all the science can begin the birds have to be caught . . .
It was our first chance to catch a glimpse of Glen's inventiveness. It also
relied heavily on him knowing his bird.

The birds tend to arrive overnight, flying at first into the lush silver-
green iris beds of the machair and then, later in the season, moving to the
denser vegetation to nest. Each male establishes his own territory and an-
nounces it to the entire island with his calling. If an intruder arrives on
his patch the established male makes haste towards the new caller.
Presumably, deep in the iris beds at night many territorial battles are
fought, won and lost. Glen and Charlie wait for darkness before setting
out to catch birds as the calling, known as 'craking', is at its most intense
after dark. Their equipment: a very bright torch to dazzle the Corncrake,
a net (like a giant butterfly net), a tape-player and a tape-recording of a
male Corncrake in full crake! And, of course, a film crew in keen but by

'Just a disembodied voice from the Iris beds'

now rather bemused pursuit. After a good walk across the machair fields we could hear the craking as Charlie pointed out the first bird they were to target.

'There's a few crakes coming from behind these rocks, I think that's our man. There's another bird craking behind.'

To which Glen replied, 'Yeah, that's him. I'll take the other guy out later!'

Ominous words directed towards a small bird which has just flown all the way from Africa to breed. The evening had all the atmosphere of a covert military operation. With the whites of their faces covered by an assortment of bobble hats, balaclavas and beards, Charlie and Glen lay down in front of the rocks, flattened themselves to the ground and turned on the tape-player. The newly arrived Corncrake craked with vigour and aplomb, the recorded bird squeaked a tinny reply. Even in the dark I could feel Chris's distaste – to him this was clearly not a Grade One bird recording. But to Corncrake ears it obviously sounded convincing and 'our man' could be heard stalking through the Iris towards the brazen plastic intruder. Charlie could only whisper his excitement in the dark: 'He's sneaking in. I can here him moving. He's going to come, he's going to come . . .'

A small partridge-like shape could just be discerned in the dark, long legs edging towards the squeaking tape-player. I don't know if male

37

Machair meadows in front of the RSPB Warden's House, Coll

Corncrakes have self esteem but I rather hoped that 'our man' hadn't caught sight of the cheap, black plastic box that had lured him out of the Iris bed as he was suddenly floodlit by the dazzling torch. With no time even for a low-level crake, the net was bought down around him. Charlie and Glen had 'our man'.

The Corncrake was taken back to the waiting Landrover where he was weighed and measured with thoroughness and care. Despite his large call, at this moment the bird seemed very small. At first he used his natural defence mechanism by playing dead, allowing his body to flop in Glen's hand and his long pink legs to dangle. But he soon perked up and took stock of his surroundings. His head in the torch light was a slate-blue colour, his wings a bright chestnut, his eyes big and brown. Once the measurements were finished, Glen glued the transmitter to his feathers, checked that it worked and he was released into the night. The process might appear traumatic but, as Glen explained, it is vital if these birds are to be saved from extinction:

> We use radio transmitters on Corncrakes to discover what they are doing because you can never see the birds them-

selves, they are always hidden in cover. This technique enables us to find out what kind of vegetation they are in, where they place their nests and how widely they range. The research itself isn't stressful to the birds, although catching them obviously is. But we've never had any problems with the birds: they seem to stay close to the same site and they breed successfully. Once the research is complete we should be able to manage the land far better for them. When studies began here we just didn't understand anything about the Corncrake, it was just a disembodied voice in the iris beds.

Keeping track: RSPB researcher Glen Tyler radio-tracking Corncrakes

Mark was delighted. With one bird carrying a transmitter he had at least a chance of making a film about the Corncrake. By keeping in close contact with Glen he would be able to establish the bird's movements and, hopefully, film some of its behaviour. He had also filmed the entire catching process, although it would be many days before we would know how successful this had been. Filming at night is always possible by using lights, but these were the very things that we had been unable to use on this occasion as the Corncrake could not have been caught if we had floodlit the machair. Instead, Mark had used a special type of film especially designed for use in very low-light conditions. In fact, the light was so low that he hadn't even been able to see through the viewfinder properly, he just had to guess at the focusing.

The Corncrake definitely keeps unsociable hours. At first light Glen wanted to track the bird and make sure of its well being. For us, one drawback with life in the Hebrides is that in summer first light follows all too rapidly from last light and, having just spent the night filming the nocturnal behaviour of the bird researchers, there was going to be no chance of sleep if we were to follow Glen and film the bird. It was a brilliant morning, one of those special dawns that make you wonder why you waste so many of life's sunrises. Glen went off to try and locate the Corncrake so we decided to film an interview with Charlie as he sat in front of his house with a mug of tea and reflected on the benefits of being the RSPB warden on Coll.

> On a morning like this it's fantastic – you can hear Snipe drumming in the background, there's a Corncrake down the bottom of the garden and there's a great sense of burgeoning spring. All the work you've done over the winter is bearing fruit and you hear the birds arriving and settling into this amazing place.

On this occasion the pictures did take second place to the sound since Charlie's interview was set against the backdrop of one of the most vibrant dawn choruses I have ever heard.

By five o'clock that morning Glen had re-located the Corncrake and was busy following him along a row of docks and nettles not far from Charlie's house. To seek out the birds Glen walks the fields carrying what appeared to be a television aerial and wearing headphones. If any bird with a transmitter attached was in range, he would soon pick up its distinctive audio signal and know exactly which bird he was following.

Coll really is a special place. The island is only 13 miles long and 3 miles wide. Low-lying machair meadows are bounded by high Marram-covered sand dunes. Like all islands, it is a safe haven for wildlife, species that are rarely seen on the mainland have a much higher profile here. The village of Arinagour is built around the island's only natural harbour, a small sea loch. It is at the pier in Arinagour that the ferry from the west coast town of Oban regularly docks. There's no air service to Coll and in winter the ferry only calls on three days of the week, but far from making the island seem isolated the lack of daily contact with mainland Scotland has bequeathed Coll with a strong sense of community.

The fact that we were working on an island was brought home to us by incidents like the 'sandwich emergency' which lasted for a few days in late spring. Keeping Mark and Chris well supplied with sandwiches may not be in the job description but it's an integral part of a producer's work. Unseasonable bad weather prevented the ferry from docking for a couple of days in May and the bread supplies in the two shops on Coll were quickly used up. Filming morale tends to drop sharply when the sandwiches run out, but on islands like Coll everyone in the community knows who bakes their own bread and who has a stock of yeast. Our filming project had great support from the people of Coll and the jam sandwiches continued to flow, despite the absence of the ferry.

Such displays of community spirit are heartening in today's world, however, it was going to be much harder for us to convey the island atmosphere to the audience of the Corncrake programme. With the arrival of a single-engine seaplane bringing day visitors from Glasgow the island was buzzing. Many Collachs were keen to have a rare, bird's-eye view of their island. Chris and Mark were no less enthusiastic. If we could film from the air, Coll's island status would be clear to anyone watching our programme.

It was a beautiful, still clear day and after phone calls to arrange insurance we were off. The take-off was rather disconcerting but once we had climbed to 800 feet the view of Coll was spectacular. It could have been a Mediterranean island below us. The sea was aquamarine and so clear that you could see seals swimming underwater along the coast. Apart from the dunes the island is, for the most part, low-lying exposed rocks and meadows. Farmhouses are widely scattered, substantial buildings joined by the narrow thread of the few miles of tarmaced road on Coll. Our aerial perspective gave us many clues as to why the island is still favoured by the Corncrake. Sheep and cattle still shelter against the walls of small fields. Their dung accumulates there which means that these well-fertilised edges and field corners become overgrown with weeds during summer. Supplemented by the RSPB's Corncrake corners and corridors the birds still have plenty of cover here in which to skulk. Farming elsewhere has basically become too clinical, too tidy for the Corncrake. As the plane turned back in across Breachacha Bay we were treated to a bird's-eye view of the castles . . .

The Isle of Coll is one of the windiest places in Britain

and there was Glen, racing along the road on his bicycle, aerial flying, hot in pursuit of yet another male Corncrake.

Once he has established a territory as his own the male Corncrake sets out to attract a female with his craking calls. Mark had been following and filming a male as he scuffled about in the undergrowth after slugs, snails and other Corncrake delicacies. He then started craking for a partner. One morning Mark was aware of another, silent, Corncrake in the vicinity: a female. She is very similar in appearance to the male but with less blue-grey on her head. The filming revealed her cautious stalk towards the male's territory. Every few yards she would raise her head above the nettles in a periscope-like fashion. When she came close enough he puffed up his gorgeous ruddy plumage and stretched his wings out, presumably to increase his body size so that it matched more nearly the size of his call. We didn't witness the mating but it was obviously successful for, within a few days, the female was settled on a nest deep in the nettles.

There are now believed to be 537 pairs of Corncrake breeding in Scotland with 25 calling males reported from Coll in 1994. Like all

rare creatures, the Corncrake is protected by special laws designed to prevent people from disturbing them. Researchers such as Glen have to be issued with special licences by Scottish Natural Heritage before they can study the Corncrake during the breeding season. Mark and Chris also needed licences for filming and sound recording.

Changes in farming practice throughout the world are believed to be the main cause of the Corncrake's dramatic decline. Apart from the decrease in suitable places to nest, the widespread use of pesticides has reduced the invertebrates on which Corncrakes feed. There has also been a change in the way that hay is grown and cut. In many areas it has been totally replaced by silage production, in others mowing takes place much earlier in the season as farmers are pressured to make land ever more productive. All ground-nesting birds are vulnerable to machinery such as mowers and harvesters, and sadly the Corncrake is no exception. Glen Tyler had already spent time in Ireland observing how the Corncrakes there react to mowers. He discovered that the Corncrake's philosophy seems to be 'Why fly when you can run? Why run when you can just sit tight and hope that danger will go away?'. This may have been a successful strategy when danger was a sharp-eyed predator with eyes keen enough to detect any sign of movement; it doesn't work when danger is a high-speed mower systematically cutting wide swathes through the machair hay. Earlier cutting and increased mechanisation in recent years means that many females on eggs and those with broods of young chicks have fallen to the mowers blades.

But although conservationists worldwide consider the Corncrake a great rarity, to many islanders they seem far more commonplace. Once again Coll farmer Alan Brodie had a Corncrake on his land. To him the Corncrake isn't a novelty.

Corncrake-friendly mowing

> You get used to having it around. It's a bit strange to see other people with binoculars and tripods peering at it. I think the Corncrakes are part of island life really. Island people have a love-hate relationship with them . . . it's not pleasant to be woken by them at four in the morning but it is nice to have them around.

Alan is one of many island farmers who sign up to the Corncrake initiative each year. Farmers in the scheme receive payment from RSPB and Scottish Natural Heritage for every male that calls consistently on their land. In return the farmers agree to continue to farm in a Corncrake-friendly manner. Because of the weather, the seasons (like much else in life here) tend to run a little late. This means that the hay has traditionally been cut later, allowing the Corncrakes to raise their young successfully before they become vulnerable to the mowing machinery. The conservationists have also introduced Corncrake-friendly mowing practices.

> At first sight it looks as if the special way you have to cut your field is going to be a bit of a hassle. But when you actually do it, it is not half as much trouble as you thought. It's really easy once you get used to it.

Rather than mowing fields from the outside towards the inside, the process is reversed. The farmer drives to the centre of the field and then, in ever-widening circles, cuts towards the field edges. If a Corncrake in the field has young, Corncrake-friendly mowing will allow her to escape with her brood towards the field edge rather than being driven towards a grim fate in the centre of the field.

There was plenty to occupy the team as everyone waited the 19 days for our female's seven green-brown eggs to hatch. Chris had placed tiny microphones in the nest and run hundreds of metres of cable back to where he could eavesdrop on the birds without disturbing them. It gave everyone a unique opportunity to listen in to activity in the nest prior to hatching. Although the female does not crake, she clearly has quite a range of quieter calls primarily used to communicate with the young chicks after hatching. What came as a surprise was that she appeared to be communicating with the chicks before they hatched from their eggs . . . and they answered!

Scientists now believe that this system of pre-hatching communication enables the hen bird to synchronise the time that her chicks will chip through their shells.

The first week of August was a tense time. Conservationists waited for eggs to hatch whilst farmers waited for the right weather and contractors to arrive on the island to begin the mowing. In the meantime there was plenty to think about as the day of the Coll show and ceilidh approached. Such occasions are a focus for island life and provide an important opportunity for conservationists and islanders to socialise. Integrating with the community is a vital part of Charlie's life on the island.

> The birds' continued presence here depends on the relationship between islanders and conservationists. The conservationists have to get on with the islanders because they want to influence the way the land is managed, but it is a two-way process in that islanders benefit from having the birds here. There are lots of Government grants targeted at the birds and those go straight into the pockets of the farmers, and there are also a lot of tourists that visit Coll because of the Corncrake.

On Friday, 5 August, the 5 a.m. ferry from Oban to Coll via Tiree was full. This was the day of the Coll show and ceilidh. Tourists and contractors jostled with show judges and musicians. The sheep-judging was the earnest part of the day, with Coll's best beasts penned up in a field across the road from the village hall. The agricultural competition was followed by games, events and side-shows. Charlie took the opportunity to explain Corncrake-friendly farming practices whilst Glen walked away with the prize for 'Best Cherry Cake'. Following the afternoon's prize-giving and inter-island football match everyone took a brief rest before the ceilidh, which was due to begin at eight. Like the seasons, social events in the Hebrides often run late but by 1 a.m. the ceilidh was in full, if sometimes unsteady, swing. As the music occasionally dipped, a constant craking call could be heard emanating from the Iris bed behind the village hall.

Once a female is settled on eggs the males return to the fields for more call duelling. Sometimes they will attract a second mate but for the most part the summer is filled with territorial defensive craking. Mark had put a canvas hide up near an old potato harvester in Brian MacIntyre's field. The entire field glowed a brilliant yellow with buttercups. Each evening as the sun set behind the wheels of the harvester the song battles would begin. Chris was not the only one keen to record the call of the Corncrake. Now that most of the birds had been caught and tagged, Glen was also busy recording their calls.

> The reason that I'm recording the sound is that we think the males might have individual voices. They can obviously tell each other apart and we can sometimes identify a bird with a particularly unusual call but we have to find a more scientific way to separate them. I record individual males throughout the

Coll's 'best beasts' at the annual show

spring and summer, my recordings are then transferred to the computer and specialist researchers at Nottingham University analyse the printouts or sonagraphs. The results already look very promising, the voices of individual birds seem to stay the same all season. If every male Corncrake does have an individual call we should be able to tell if the same birds are returning to exactly the same spot without needing to re-catch them every year.

Although most island farmers have adopted the new method of Corncrake-friendly mowing Charlie and Glen were keen to monitor any mowing near a nest. The exact mowing time is dependent on weather and contractors, and is therefore difficult for farmers to predict. If we were to watch and film mowing taking place, we all needed to keep an early-morning eye out to see which farmer was going to be mowing near which nest. The best solution seemed to be for someone to be out before dawn to spot any activity and then wake the others. We formed a plan . . . I was to sleep in the car parked at a good vantage point and wake all the others as soon as mowing began. I set my alarm for dawn and snuggled

Why fly when you can walk?

into my sleeping bag, thankful that mowing takes place in August, not November!

Half an hour after sunrise the tractors began to rumble into action. I called at Charlie's house and left him to wake Glen and then dashed back to the Coll Hotel to wake Mark and Chris; it was far too early to phone. The hotel was locked and the master plan rapidly began to fail. As I couldn't creep in and tap on their doors to rouse them I had to work out which windows of the rambling building related to the rooms that Mark and Chris were occupying. The window of what I thought was Chris's room was open, so I started calling out to him. I dared not shout loudly as Chris's wife, Maggie, their twin sons, Alex and Lewis, and daughter, Rosie, had come over to join him for a brief holiday. Silence. Next, I threw small stones through the open window but still no response. The thought briefly crossed my mind that I might be caught throwing stones through the window of an innocent tourist. Most unusual activities connected with filming can be explained, but throwing stones through someone's window at 3.30 a.m. might prove difficult to pass off as essential behaviour for a film producer. I decided to try Mark.

Mark's room was at the back of the hotel above a low, slightly sloping, slate roof. It was definitely Mark's room because of the empty film boxes that adorned the sill, but it was shut. At this rate the mowing would be finished by the time we were in action. I had to get to the window and tap on it. I climbed on to the slates via a pile of empty bottle crates and as I wriggled up towards the window I focused firmly on the film boxes, not daring to look down. I repeatedly called out to Mark as I progressed up the slates – if he woke and came to the window I would be able to climb in – I was hoping to leave the hotel by a more conventional route. Mark was finally roused but I think the rest of the hotel may well have been too – my grip had failed about a foot below the window ledge and I slid backwards off the slates landing eventually and uncomfortably in the crates. I am always rather amused by people's frequent comment when I explain that I am a television producer, 'Oh, what a glamorous job!'. They really have no idea . . .

Finally we were all assembled in the hay field as the mowing began. At this early stage the Corncrake and her recently hatched brood were oblivious to proceedings. At least her eggs had hatched and she could move the chicks; eggs are far more vulnerable which is why farmers are encouraged to leave their mowing as late as possible. Glen knew the exact whereabouts of the nest but he could only guess the birds' reaction as the mower drew closer. By careful watching and close communication with the farmer the hen Corncrake and her brood made it safely to the rough grass at the edge of the field. Here they should be safe, away from the machinery and covered from the eyes of the predatory gulls that cruise the tops of the Cow Parsley, hungry for vulnerable chicks. There was only one casualty that morning . . . the Corncrake was safe but the mower had not proved as friendly to Chris's microphone lead. It had been left in place, running through the hay to the nest. That afternoon as he gathered together the now rather shortened lengths he said to me, 'What a day! And Rosie didn't sleep too well. She complained in the early hours that someone was throwing stones through our bedroom window!'

Covered in black fluffy down Corncrake chicks face many risks in the few short weeks before they grow their adult feathers and fly away from Coll to Africa. Gulls will easily take an unguarded chick but so, too, will Otters, Hedgehogs and rodents. Hedgehogs were introduced to Coll and have now spread throughout the island. Like the Corncrakes, they benefit from the lack of pesticides that elsewhere control slugs and snails. The domestic cat is also a serious threat to Corncrakes. At one time many island cats were fitted with bells to warn the birds off. As is so often the way with nature the reverse happened. Usually shy and skulking, the Corncrakes were curious about this strange tinkling sound and ploughed through the vegetation to search out the bells. For a brief while the hunting life of the cats of Coll became a little to easy.

Just one last task remained before the Corncrakes left the island and Glen could migrate back to RSPB headquarters. The Corncrake chicks had to be caught and tiny numbered rings put around their legs so that they could be identified in future years. The female does not keep her brood in the nest for long once they have hatched, there are too many

Corncrake chick

tell-tale signs and smells for predators in its vicinity. Mark filmed one hen carefully lifting pieces of broken eggshell and carrying them away from the nest. So as soon as the chicks can walk she leads them away from this potentially dangerous area. Chris sat close by one nest with what looked like a satellite dish. It was a parabolic reflector, specially designed to pick up sounds from a wide area and funnel them into the microphone. As the chicks spread out through the machair meadow, quickly learning to feed for themselves, Chris recorded their cheeps. The hen followed them closely, constantly alert. At the first hint of danger she uttered a low chicken-like chuckle and the chicks would run back to her side. It was the first time that such a call had ever been recorded.

Glen, inventive as ever, had devised a way to catch the chicks. Once a brood had been located in the tall grass he and Charlie erected two long, fine nets to form a funnel-shaped barricade on the ground in front of the chicks. Charlie remained behind the nets while Glen patrolled the ground behind the chicks. He moved slowly to and thro, taking care not to tread on any of the youngsters but his footsteps alone would not have been enough to urge the chicks forwards. As he moved, he gently swayed the tape player across the grass tops. This time he was playing a different recording, one of an ancient tractor mowing! A sound sure to drive young

Corncrakes away! As Glen moved towards the nets with the tape spluttering and squeaking, the chicks scuttled through the long grass and fell into the net. Charlie swiftly removed them and they were soon weighed, measured and ringed. They were quickly released back into the cover of the grass and as we watched them go it was hard to believe that these tiny birds would be capable of flying all the way to Southern Africa in just five weeks. But for Glen the summer's work had all been worthwhile,

Glen Tyler and RSPB Warden Charlie Self ringing Corncrake chicks

> Their future in Scotland is now looking quite good after a period when it looked terrible. It seemed like they really were going to become extinct. They will remain scarce over most of the country but there are areas like the Hebrides where the habitat remains suitable and can be improved, like it is at the moment. There's a glimmer that it's looking secure here ... but they'll never be common again over the whole of Scotland.

Information gained from the research is already being put into practice and the year following our filming the numbers of calling Corncrakes on Coll rose yet again to 37, with birds nesting on both the reserve and neighbouring farmland. With a great deal of patience and care Mark had managed to film unique events in the Corncrake calendar with close-up shots of the bird in full crake so that you could see it's breast feathers rippling with the effort of the call. Even Chris had to agree that the pictures added something to his soundtrack, but it was a memorable film for him, too. Never before had he included so many bird calls in one film, from the shrill alarm of the Dunlin, to the piping call of the Oyster-catcher; Snipe drum with fervour and gulls cry as they wheel overhead and then, of course, recorded for certain posterity is that unmistakable call of Coll – the Corncrake.

CHAPTER THREE

WILD WOODS

The wild woods of Scotland are magical places, full of atmosphere and life. To walk alone deep in the forest is an awe-inspiring experience. On even the calmest of days the huge Scots Pine trees seem to whisper with anticipation.

The Caledonian pine forest is full of surprises. Dominated by the coniferous Scots Pines, you might expect it to be a dark and gloomy place. Instead, dappled light of many colours filters through gaps in the trees to the forest floor. As the sun moves across the sky, the patterns on the floor drift and change like a giant kaleidoscope. Coniferous forests have a reputation for being sterile, lifeless woods where little grows but the camera's lens is quick to focus your powers of observation. We began to notice the small details of forest life and realised that each season in the pine forest has something new to show: spiders trailing silver web lines off fresh green Birch leaves; a carpet of gentle pink Twinflower; or the burgundy reds and burnished golds of fungi in autumn. Even in midwinter the forest is very definitely alive.

The once great wood of Caledon used to cover much of Scotland, now only scattered remnants of the mighty forest remain but these are like islands in the bare glens, providing a safe haven for many of Scotland's most famous species. Our attention is often focused on such creatures – neither the appeal nor the plight of the Golden Eagle or Scottish Wildcat can easily be ignored – but it is also important to see and understand the environment that supports them. Natural history television programmes also tend to concentrate on individual animals: 'figurehead' species; often cute, cuddly or threatened wildlife that will keep our attention and win our support. The danger of such programmes is that they may create the impression that the animals exist in isolation, *Operation Survival* aimed to reflect the complete tableaux of Scotland's wildlife heritage and that included people and habitats as well as the cute and cuddlies! The forest already had me captivated, now I just had to persuade the team . . .

Filming tends to begin in early spring so that the complete wildlife year can be portrayed and, following our February filming trip to Coll, Mark decided to spend some time in the RSPB-owned Abernethy Forest on Speyside. In the first few days he began to doubt whether Coll really was the windiest place in Britain. We were hoping to film winter's end, the snow melting and the forest bursting with spring activity, but in early March winter was still the active season on Speyside. From his lodgings, Mark watched the snow falling and plaintively assured me that there was nothing much going on out there anyway. But, like all wildlife film-makers, he would not be confined to quarters long and when he did venture into the sleet-driven forest he found that the wildlife was continuing with its own timetable, despite the weather. Crossbills were busy using their strange specialised beaks to prise out the kernels from pine cones. Small flocks of these bright-red and grey or yellow and grey birds flew between the pine tops. Until recently it was believed that the red and yellow colour distinguished the sexes, males are red and females are yellow but recent genetic studies have cast doubt on the theory. Now it appears that females may also have red plumage.

As the birds continued their search the sun came out and by the end of the day the trees sparkled with droplets of melting snow. We still had another three seasons of filming left, yet Mark was well on his way to illustrating the magic of the forest for *Operation Survival*.

Our main challenge was deciding exactly what to include in the forest film. After a few weeks' research I felt we could make an entire series devoted to forest wildlife and the efforts being made by people to preserve it. Because time was limited, we needed to focus on just a few species that would still give an intimation of the sheer diversity of life in the forest. Red Squirrels have been in Scotland since the forests became established here at the end of the last Ice Age, 10,000 years ago. The Red Squirrel has declined dramatically in other parts of Britain since its cousin, the Grey Squirrel, was introduced from America two hundred years ago, but in Scotland the population is stable. The filming of any wild animal or plant takes a great deal of forethought and planning. The filming team, and particularly the cameraman, need to be good naturalists with as much knowledge of the animal's behaviour as possible. Only then can you predict when will be the best time to film. Red Squirrels are notoriously shy but Mark knew of a place on the forest edge where they came out regularly to feed. He set up his small canvas hide and waited.

Red Squirrels spend most of their time feeding on pine kernels: the forest floor is often littered with the well-chewed evidence of pine cones stripped and discarded like apple cores. The cones ripen in autumn but the seeds do not fall to the ground until spring, providing both squirrels and crossbills with a tree-top food supply throughout the winter. One morning in early spring the squirrels were searching for food on the ground, accompanied by a flock of Chaffinches. If any of these bright birds strayed too close, the foraging squirrel would sit up and chatter angrily at it with a churring call accompanied by a shivering and thrashing of the tail. As Mark filmed the interaction between the two species, he felt something brushing repeatedly against his feet. He looked down to see that a Red Squirrel had squeezed itself under the canvas hide and was now busy helping itself to the peanuts he had brought to tempt them with. If only all wildlife was this obliging!

*Red Squirrels arrived in Scotland
at the end of the last ice age, at the
same time as the Scots Pine*

Many of the Scots Pine trees in the forest are of a great age, we
counted the growth rings of a fallen pine and it is clear that they may live
for in excess of three hundred years. These trees provide a living link with
history, many were big enough to shelter soldiers fleeing from the Battle
of Culloden 250 years ago. Highland history seems to pervade every
corner of the forest; on a quiet evening it is tempting to believe that you
can still hear the howl of the Wolves that once roamed here. But much
has changed in the forest since the last Wolf was shot in 1743. Many of
the other large animals – bears, Lynx and Elk – had become extinct in the
preceding centuries, the wild Boar had disappeared a hundred years

It's tempting to believe you can still hear the howls of Wolves

before the Wolf and by the beginning of the seventeenth century the forests themselves were vanishing.

Peter Wormell is a conservationist who has spent many years in the forest revelling in the atmosphere created by the ancient trees. Concerned by the loss of the forest Peter established a native tree nursery which he replenishes with seeds collected from the wild. He gathers pine seed in early spring when the new season's warmth bursts the cones and releases the seed which falls to the ground. Occasionally Peter needs to climb the trees to collect the cones before they open but even a tricky climb doesn't dull his enthusiasm for the forest.

> The pinewoods are such a fine setting to work in and the weather doesn't matter too much as long as its not a blizzard. One of the greatest pleasures of all is to be at the top of a pine tree – if you climb out on to the top branches on a good clear crisp day, you get an incredible view. Sometimes you can see eagles flying and a crossbill will come and gather seed along with you just a few feet away. It's a world on its own.

Native Scots Pine seed is highly valuable but the gathering involves time and a good deal of hard walking and climbing. Peter has a regular team of collectors, mainly retired people, who all seem to look forward to the spring task.

> It's just a pleasant day out. Margaret's minibus provides the transport and she usually does a bit of home-baking. We sip our soup and just enjoy the environment of the pinewoods. They have such a distinctive feel about them; its the antiquity of them, the ancient feel of the old trees.

A fine day out in the forest collecting pine cones

The gathering team have permission to collect in specific areas of native forest. In late March they were due to visit the ancient pinewood of Doire Darach near the Bridge of Orchy. We planned to join them but winter was tenacious. Every time we arranged a date and set out from our Aberdeen base snow blocked the route to Glen Orchy. Finally, on 29 April, long after the seeds were ready for collecting, we all managed to beat the weather and drive up to the small patch of forest. We weren't the only ones to have been affected by the violent snow storms during the early spring. Many of the older trees had been badly battered. We filmed the team as they walked through the forest gathering cones from the easily accessible fallen branches. As he picked, Peter explained the history of Doire Darach.

> The last big felling here was towards the end of the eighteenth century when some Irishmen came over and cut all the trees. It's recorded in the parish statistical account that the trees were logged down the Orchy river to Loch Awe where they were hewn into hulks of wood, carted down to Loch Etive and shipped away. It was apparently done without the consent of the Laird, they were just Irish adventurers.

The adventurers left only the twisted trees that would provide poor quality timbers. Today many of these gnarled trees have become the splendid so-called 'granny pines' of the forest. At the base of the tree the bark is silver-grey but as the trunk twists up through the laden branches its bark becomes a salmon-pink that seems to flame orange in the setting sun. Despite their great age, the granny pines continue to produce cones but the forest's natural regeneration is a slow process and Doire Darach, like so many of Scotland's plundered forests, was never replanted. 'Doire Darach' is Gaelic for 'thicket of oak', and although Caledonian pine forest is dominated by Scots Pine, it is naturally a mixed forest with patches of other tree species. Birch should flourish in damper areas, with a patchwork of Rowan and Juniper, Oak and Aspen occurring elsewhere. Aspen is one of Scotland's least known forest trees with its thin long stalked leaves that seem to shiver and tremble in the breeze. In Gaelic it is *eubh* or *cran* critheanach: 'the shaking tree'.

The history of Scotland's wild woods is enough to produce a shiver. For thousands of years people lived on the forest edge, using wood coppiced from trees on its perimeter and collecting fungi, nuts and berries without needing to venture far into or exploit the forest interior. But with the industrial revolution the demand for timber became insatiable, many trees were taken for charcoal production. English-based iron smelters set up foundries in Scotland, foundries that were to be fed by the Caledonian forest. Huge quantities of sawn logs were required for ship building, a demand that was increased by three centuries of European and World wars. Some tree species are capable of recovering from even fairly substantial large-scale harvesting – broadleaved trees such as Aspen can grow new shoots from the cut stump – but the Scots Pine can only reproduce itself from seed. Once sheep numbers increased in the eighteenth century and the Red Deer population began to grow, few pine saplings could survive the insistent attacks from their grazing muzzles.

Although the pine forests have declined, the Scots Pine tree is, despite its method of reproduction, a natural survivor. Along with Juniper and Yew, it is one of only three coniferous trees that occur naturally in Britain. Scots pine grows from the Pacific right across Europe, surviving at altitudes of 2,400 metres and often growing from what appears to be a bare rock face. The seeds are also hardy. Peter Wormell kept some in his refrigerator for 15 years and yet they germinated and have been successfully planted out on his nursery. He is always careful to mark the exact origin of the seed as recent genetic studies have shown that Scots Pine trees can vary from district to district and glen to glen.

Graham Tuley of the Forestry Authority has spent many years studying Scotland's pine forests, which he compares to the rainforests of the Amazon.

> Everyone talks about the tropical rainforest but we have our own temperate rainforest here which is much more threatened than many of the tropical ones. The forest was much better in the past before man killed many of the large animals. It's now only a relic of it's former glory but perhaps with encouragement over the next couple of hundred years we can get back something of the splendour that used to be in Scotland a few thousand years ago.

In recent years Graham has spent much of his time wandering remote glens with a tape measure, sizing up the trees as part of a major inventory of native pine woods,

> This is the first survey of pinewoods for 40 years and it was discovered that we actually have about 16,000 hectares scattered throughout the northern part of Scotland.

In fact, the forestry team found that there was more forest left than anyone realised. The project, which involved surveying and mapping any woodland with more than 30 trees, uncovered 3,500 hectares of previously unrecorded pine forest. The new inventory will provide a valuable basis for further research on all aspects of forest management.

Man has been manipulating the forests for thousands of
years but the last two World Wars decimated large areas. It
will be a long time before we've recreated reasonable forest
over Scotland and I don't think we should cover the whole
country with trees. What I'm interested in is what it's going
to be like in 200 years' time. My immediate priority is to
establish seed sources in remote areas so that the next
generation of foresters have something better to work.

Peter Wormell is already benefiting from the pine saplings he planted 15
years ago. The trees are already bearing cones and, as they are only 15 feet
high, it's a lot easier for him to collect them than cones from the granny
pines in forests like Doire Darach.

The Red Squirrels had been particularly obliging but we antipated
that many forest creatures would be more difficult to film. Both the
Pine Marten and the Wildcat were likely to prove elusive but Mark and
I also felt that we should try and film some of the less predictable

woodland creatures: bats, for instance. Bats tend to be regarded as urban animals, roosting and hibernating in buildings, but as Mick Canum, a Forestry Commission Wildlife Officer explained to me, bats were originally woodland dwellers, squeezing into the nooks and crevices of decaying trees. They have only moved as their natural forest homes have been destroyed. Mick is involved in a Forestry Commission project to encourage bats back to the trees. The key to a healthy forest is variety, and bats like a mixture of live trees, which support a good insect population for food, and dead, rotting trees with plenty of holes for roosting. Young trees in the new forestry plantations do not offer the same cosy corners in which bats can hide away, so Mick has been providing alternative roosting sites with a network of bat boxes. We joined him as he climbed high into a Scots Pine in Speyside to check one of these boxes. Carefully, Mick lifted the lid of the box and removed the tiny gremlin-faced creature, placing it in a dark cotton bag before taking it down to the ground for a more thorough inspection.

It's a Pipistrelle, a male Pipistrelle. This is our smallest bat species. I was expecting to get Daubenton's Bat here because we are beside a loch and they feed on aquatic insects. Pipistrelles tend to feed on smaller insects like midges. He is a real surprise find because at this time of the year male bats are normally setting up harems – mating roosts where males recruit females – and this one is all on his own. He's obviously missed out!

Once the Pipistrelle had been checked over and his vital statistics recorded, Mick released him. The bat did one brief circuit of the clearing before flying off into the pines.

There are now bat boxes in 30 forest sites throughout the north of Scotland, from Caithness to Kintyre. The specially designed boxes, such as 'The Tanglewood Wedge', have a gap just big enough to allow a bat to squeeze through without letting in unwelcome visitors like the Red Squirrel. Squirrels are omnivorous and will readily add bats and young birds to their diet of pine seeds. All four of the bat species that occur in northern Scotland – Pipistrelle, Daubenton's, Brown Long-Eared and Natterer's – have been declining in recent years, mainly as a result of the increased use of pesticides and the destruction of their roost sites. But regular monitoring of the boxes may provide scientists like Mick with enough information about bats to reverse the decline.

Scientists can also record the sex of the bats using the boxes, whether it's males using them as harems or females using them as maternity roosts, or if they are just intermediate resting places rather than major roost sites. All four species use the boxes, although Daubenton's are the least common, and we now have a far better understanding of how the species are distributed. And it's not just bats that benefit from the boxes, they are also used by birds such as Treecreepers.

Apart from inspecting the boxes, Mick also identifies bats on their evening flights with a 'bat detector'. All British bats are very small and usually only begin to fly at dusk. Because of the low light and their size it's usually impossible to identify bats by eye but, like dolphins, bats use echo-locating clicks to navigate and locate their prey. Young people, or sound recordists, with very sharp hearing, can sometimes pick out the bat's clicks but the hand-held detector magnifies inaudible clicks. Different species of bat use different frequencies for their echo-locating calls. As a bat flies over, a dial on the front of the detector, which looks like a sophisticated pocket compass, tells Mick the frequency of the bat's call and allows him to identify the species. Pipistrelle Bats, for instance, use either 45 or 55 kilohertz for their clicks.

Each patch of Caledonian forest, whether large or small, seems to have its own individual character. On the east coast much of the remaining forest still stands in large dense blocks, like the woodlands of Deeside, while the west-coast forests are usually smaller, with more scattered trees, like Doire Darach. The Glen Affric Forest Reserve is one of my favourite woodlands. Within an easy drive of Inverness the reserve still feels remote; the sort of forest where it is possible to walk for hours without seeing or

The tourist myth, a landscape
bereft of trees

hearing another human being. Despite the beauty of its forests Scotland does not have the image of being a heavily wooded land, the tourist depiction is of an open landscape dominated by heather-covered hills. For many years Ron Greer, a Glaswegian, has campaigned against the promotion of a landscape that is bereft of trees.

> Natural it's not. Tourist myth it is. It's actually a mess, an ecological slum. Both metaphorically and literally it's a ruin based on the destruction of the whole natural forest ecosystem and a way of life for human beings who interacted with that forest for about 9,000 years.

Ron Greer rarely minces his words. Standing in the ruin of an ancient summer shieling on the shore of Loch Garry, he pondered what its original occupants might think of today's tree-bare hills.

> I wonder what would happen if the people who used to live in this wee summer village could come back today and see this empty landscape. What would they think? I'm sure they

would be just as angry as I am. Why aren't there any people here during the summer any more? There's no one living in wee villages like this one along the lochside or along other glens that run into the area. It's hard for us now to imagine that there was once a bustling way of life here that gave people a reasonable standard of living for the times. Those people would be shocked at the emptiness of the country, why there's so many sheep, so few cattle.

Sheep, Ron passionately feels, are at the very core of the problem faced by Scotland's forests. During the production of *Operation Survival* I began to notice how many conservation issues seem to come back to the problems created by just two animals and their management: sheep and Red Deer. After ten minutes of filming with Ron it was clear that he would gladly remove every sheep from the Highlands. That being impossible, not to say illegal, even for a man of Ron's endless energy, he has set himself a slightly lesser goal . . . to replant as much forest as humanly possible. In the early days of his campaign he made solitary visits to Loch Garry to replant trees when and where he could, using his savings to pay for the fencing that would protect the precious saplings from grazing sheep.

Ron Greer – a man determined to replant the once great wood of Caledon

> That limited area of fencing was worth it to me . . . I don't know if the bank manager agrees! It's surprising what you can get out of this environment, the bleakness is a creation of our own. It's really quite an easy job to get the trees going once you get the fencing sorted out because it's the grazing which is the problem, not the climate.

His passion is infectious and in 1986 Ron established the Loch Garry Tree Group, volunteers who meet up at weekends to plant trees. The group has no particular affiliations, it's just a gathering of people who want to see more trees in the Highlands.

> The Tree Group is a small organisation with a big task but we are getting off our backsides and actually doing the work, and the unit benefit per money spent here is obvious. My vision is that by the time I've retired these children will have grown up and be bringing their children and we'll have this whole loch surrounded in a mixed deciduous forest the way it was hundreds of years ago. And that forest will be the creation, not of some bureaucratic whim, but of ordinary local people of all different kinds of professional and working backgrounds. It'll be a forest built with their hearts and hands and minds and their own resources . . . and that's significant.

Ron Greer's dream is not only to have a forested landscape but for that forest to be the basis of a local culture and economy once again. In some areas that is already beginning to happen. The Girvan family live near

A future for the Forests – Lyndsey Girvan found charcoal-making free of European bureaucracy

Drumnadrochit in a well-forested area just below Glen Affric. An established farmer, Lyndsey Girvan recently decided that with proper management the surrounding woodland could provide a boost to the family income. Although industrial charcoal manufacture played a part in the devastation of Scotland's forests, small-scale charcoal production for the barbecue market could be an important element of future forest usage. Landowners are inevitably more likely to maintain their forests if they can reap an economic harvest from them. Lyndsey Girvan also found charcoal making refreshingly free of European bureaucracy.

> It's a challenge I enjoy and we won't go beyond a level that we can't sustain. There's a lot of young trees coming on and we've already started planting some broadleaves. As a hill farmer with livestock we are very dependent on subsidy and this is something that is totally unsubsidised. It's something we're doing for ourselves, we've no interference from any bureaucratic authority, apart from satisfying the Forestry Commission over a felling licence.

After centuries of depletion, life is returning to Scotland's forests, and not just human life. The Capercaillie is a very strange bird, about the same size and similar in stance to a turkey. Capercaillie were once common in the pine forest; the bird actually eats the thin and sharp-ended pine needles. But the Capercaillie's large and somewhat rotund figures made them easy targets for the sporting guns of the eighteenth century and the last pair of Capercaillie were shot for a wedding feast at Balmoral in 1785. Fortunately, many survived in the forests of Sweden and eventually the birds were successfully reintroduced to Scotland. Their name derives from the Gaelic capull-choille or 'horse of the woods' after the strange 'clip-clopping' sound produced by the male when he is displaying. The Capercaillie display is a fantastic sight, like some ancient tribal ritual, which takes place at first light on spring mornings in the forest. The birds, both hens and cocks, gather at a 'lek site' or display ground for the contest. The hens sit demurely around the edge of the arena, like so many serene Spanish ladies, peering at a bullfight from behind their fans. Then a cock struts into view, his black tail spread open and neck stretched out as he utters a series of deep clicks and throaty pops. As he prances and leaps into the air other cocks will be drawn to the challenge, which may end in a fatal fight. The male Capercaillie is not a coy bird, once he has established his dominance at a lek he will defend his hard-won territory with vigour. These birds are frightened of no man . . . or film crew, as *Operation Survival* sound recordist Phil Croal discovered. Phil was standing in the forest with a small team of people as they discussed how best to film the antics of a particularly aggressive bird which was fiercely defending his forest domain. With no warning Phil was singled out for an attack. Perhaps it was the large furry grey microphone on the end of a long pole that so offended the bird, Phil will never know. One moment he was upright, an innocent bystander, the next he was flat on his back with a fully grown Capercaillie cock clinging to his chest.

Cock Capercaillie – not a coy bird

Despite the stories of repeated attacks by an aggressive male Capercaillie in Abernethy Forest, Mark was determined to film the creature. The bird had launched itself into the air in fury as a friend of Mark's tried to establish it's exact whereabouts, but when Mark himself arrived and set up camp in front of it, it remained passive, performing perfectly for his camera, strutting and clucking with unusually calm dignity. Perhaps it realised that in this determined wildlife cameraman it had finally met its match.

The Capercaillie has become re-established in a number of forest areas but it is still one of the rarest of British birds. Reintroducing a species to its original country can be successful but such schemes are usually fraught with countryside politics and debate. The Capercaillie became extinct

The forests are magical places full of atmosphere

because of its popularity as a game bird, few people (other than sound recordists!) were ever seriously threatened by Capercaillie. The Wolf, however, is a very different matter. It became extinct for a very different reason: fear. Conservation talk often turns to which other extinct species may in time be reintroduced to Scotland's forests. The Wolf is probably the most evocative of native Scottish forest animals but its reintroduction would, most people think, make the woodlands of Scotland feel a little too wild. However, plans are afoot to re-introduce the Beaver in the not too distant future. Not the magnificent dam-building Beaver of North America but its less ambitious European cousin.

Fortunately, attitudes towards nature have begun to change. In the years that I have been making wildlife films I have seen a distinct shift towards the view that it is far better to ensure the future of wildlife before it dies out than to try and re-introduce it after it has gone. People are increasingly aware of the fullness and diversity of nature. During autumn in the forests it is hard to escape the richness of woodland life; trees are gilded and fruits glow. More than 1,500 types of fungi grow, some of which are actually poisonous and only a few are edible.

In early September Mark went back into Abernethy to film the forest in its autumnal flush. He was particularly fascinated by the fungi growing over old tree stumps in waxy piles. Fragile opaque parasols protrude through the moss-covered forest floor; the more you look the more fungi

you see. As he filmed Mark realised that many of them looked good enough to eat. He was staying at the house of some friends while they were away and, as I was back at base in Aberdeen, he was self-catering. Often spending from dawn until gone dusk outside, shopping and domestic arrangements are not high on a cameraman's list of priorities, but here was free food and lots of it. Mark collected some fungi and took them back for a good fry up.

Fly Agaric – colourful but not edible

At 11 p.m. my phone rang. Mark often rings in the evening to update me on the day's filming. From his cheery tone I could tell it had been a good day. Then he described his evening meal and my mind became full of niggling doubts. Mark is an excellent field naturalist . . . it is an integral part of his work, but identifying those fungi which are safe to eat can be very tricky . . . I just hoped that we would have Mark as a cameraman for the next series of *Operation Survival*. I was very relieved to hear Mark when my phone rang next morning.

Although most of the larger forest creatures have become extinct, many smaller ones are still being discovered. Some of Britain's rarest species of moths, butterflies, dragonflies and beetles are only found in Scotland's native pinewoods. Four species of fly never before seen in Britain have recently been discovered in Abernethy Forest Reserve. Many of these invertebrates are dependent on the birch wood in the Caledonian forest for their survival. We met up with Diana Gilbert from an

Gilded trees and glowing fruits

organisation called Highland Birchwoods, as she examined an iridescent blue beetle wandering across the ground beneath a fallen birch.

> Birch is a vital part of the Caledonian Forest, it's one of the oldest trees in Britain and very often it is the most common in woodland. Because of its age quite a lot of invertebrates have developed to rely on it. In fact, two thirds of the moth species in Britain are found in Scottish birch woods. And yet birch is undervalued and often considered a weed. It is not managed to produce either valuable timber or a wildlife resource.

But Highland Birchwood's plan is to change all that. The organisation was set up in 1992 to provide advice and guidance to owners of woodland and is funded by Scottish Natural Heritage, the Forestry Authority, Highland Regional Council and Highlands and Islands Enterprise. The team is based just outside Inverness and offers advice on the best way to manage birch woodlands but it is also keen to promote outlets for woodland products and timber. Even small diameter pieces of wood can be used for making baskets, buckets and even boomerangs for export. Birch always looks so slender and fragile that many people would not consider it for more substantial woodcraft yet its whitish wood makes hard-wearing floors and furniture with a unique opaque appearance. With the increased concern over the use of tropical hardwoods, the sustainable use of birch could be saving two forests for future generations; native and tropical.

On our final filming trip to Glen Affric we were accompanied by retired forester Finlay Macrae and Jimmy Oswald who was, until recently, the head keeper of the Glen Tanar estate. As we climbed through Glen Affric the two men considered their lives in the forest. Finlay spent 25 years as a forester in Glen Affric.

Finlay Macrae and Jimmy Oswald enjoying the atmosphere of the Caledonian Forest

> People often talk as if the old Caledonian pine forest was some kind of gloomy place that you walked through and never saw God's light until you came out at the other end, but I think the original forest was probably very colourful. The colours in the pinewood come from the mix, you see, Birch and Rowan and Blaeberry, and so the cycle goes on. It's great to see it all coming back. I think the great value of this is that you can take it in with your own eyes. What you feel through your system, if you've lived in this sort of forest all your days, can do something for you that commercial forestry can never do.

Jimmy Oswald agreed.

> What more could a man want than this? Just look at that old granny pine there. To me it's got something that no other tree has. It is such an excellent thing to be beside because, here in this tree is probably 230 years of history. The thing I enjoy so much about this natural forest is the edge of the forest – it's ragged as the young trees regenerate up the hillside; there's no straight lines. It's just really nice being here, listening to the wind going through those trees, and it's so placid and peaceful. Therapy – even to old men like us!

It was fascinating to see that, even after so many years spent in the forest, on a bright autumnal day Jimmy and Finlay were still completely enthralled by the magic of the wild woods.

CHAPTER FOUR

BACK TO A FUTURE

The White-tailed Sea Eagle is an awesome bird. Fully grown adults have a wingspan of almost three metres and their bright-yellow feet are the size of a man's hand. When a sea eagle flies over, you don't need to see it, you can feel its presence in the air. It's little wonder that the sea eagle became central to many of the myths of northern lands. Known in Gaelic as *Iolaire sul-na Grein*, 'the eagle with the sunlit eye', the image of the sea eagle is a recurring theme in both the archaeology and art of Scotland. John Love of Scottish Natural Heritage has spent many years researching the legends that are associated with the White-tailed Sea Eagle; tales that are closely interwoven with the very fabric of Scottish history.

> These birds are very much part of the culture and history of Scotland, from recent times going way back into the past. They are mentioned in Gaelic poetry, they feature on Pictish symbol stones – such as the one found at the Knowe of Burrian on Orkney – and there are some wonderful phrases in Anglo-Saxon poetry describing the birds feeding on corpses after a battle: 'the grey coated eagle, white tailed, to have his will of the corpses'. They've been very much a feature of the whole place and its culture for hundreds of years.

But despite their central role in prehistory, by the late eighteenth century the sea eagle was regarded by many as an unwelcome feature of the Scottish landscape. Sheep farming in the Highlands had become big business and by the Victorian era many estates were being managed for game species such as Red Grouse and Arctic Hare. Golden Eagles, Wildcats, White-tailed Sea Eagles . . . all predators were destroyed with a vengeance. By searching through the accounts of nineteenth-century naturalists and the vermin records of sporting estates, John Love has built up a sad picture of the demise of the sea eagle in Scotland.

Here's a vermin list for one shooting estate in the 1830s.

John Love from SNH has built up a sad picture of the Sea Eagles demise in Scotland

Over three years it records that 27 sea eagles were killed – either shot or poisoned – in just 21 square miles, and that's just the tip of the iceberg. It was only when the human population of the Highlands began to increase (it peaked in the 1840s) that sea eagles began to be affected. Sea eagles are big, obvious birds. They are dramatic and noisy, and people would have been only too aware if they were nesting nearby. The sea eagle is also much less afraid of people than the Golden Eagle. If you go to a Golden Eagle nest the adult birds disappear and you don't see them again but sea eagles will fly around the nest calling at you. They could easily be picked off, shot, and this is why the sea eagle was so vulnerable to persecution and why the Golden Eagle, a shyer bird, was able to linger on.

As the name suggests, the White-tailed Sea Eagle bred mainly in coastal areas, although the birds were occasionally seen inland. As the eagles on the mainland were shot and poisoned out of existence, the islands of the Hebrides, Orkney and Shetland became a retreat for the species. In 1871 one writer noted that 'all the bold headlands of Skye had their pair' and shepherds reported as many as 40 sea eagles feeding off a sheep carcass. But even in these island strongholds the sea eagle was sought out. Here they were vulnerable to the attentions of Victorian trophy hunters and egg collectors. The last pair is said to have bred on Skye in 1916. A solitary albino female had survived in Shetland but in 1918 she, too, was shot. The White-tailed Sea Eagle was extinct in Scotland.

The story of the White-tailed Sea Eagle encapsulates so many features that are pertinent to the natural history of many Scottish species that we had to consider the possibility of making an *Operation Survival* film about the bird. Mark mused . . . he had successfully made a film about the Corncrake, a bird that couldn't be seen, so it was obvious . . . my next task for him would be to make a film about a bird that had actually become extinct! But thanks to a major conservation exercise that has taken place over the last 20 years this wasn't such an impossible mission. Despite the persecution that took place earlier this century, the White-tailed Sea Eagle is once again breeding on Scotland's west coast.

In the 1960s and '70s sea eagles were threatened throughout Europe. The hunting of sea eagles had already been banned in many countries but, like many other predators at the top of the food chain, sea eagles were slowly being poisoned out of existence by the increasing use of pesticides and chemical pollutants. At least Scotland was considered to be relatively pollution-free and attitudes to predators were beginning to change. The Capercaillie had been successfully reintroduced from Scandinavia, so why not the sea eagle? In 1959 three Scandinavian sea eagles were released in Argyll. In 1968 another attempt was made to re-establish the sea eagle when four Norwegian birds were released on the remote island of Fair Isle. Neither attempt brought long-term success.

John Love's interest in the sea eagle began in 1975 when he became

involved in a further attempt to re-introduce the birds. This time the Isle of Rum, a National Nature Reserve, was selected as the release site. There was a plentiful supply of natural prey for the young eagles on Rum – Red Deer, feral goats, fish and sea birds – and the island's reserve status would ensure that there would be little human disturbance.

White-tailed Sea Eagles had been protected in Norway since 1968 and by 1975 the population there was healthy. So, with the full agreement of the Norwegian authorities, a team from the Nature Conservancy Council (now Scottish Natural Heritage) flew to Norway to collect four sea eagle chicks.

Twenty years on the sea eagle project is still in operation. Today it is run by Scottish Natural Heritage and the Royal Society for the Protection of Birds. Since the project began 108 sea eagles have been released. Despite its powerful wings, the sea eagle is not a long-distance traveller, and I was surprised to discover that sea eagles do not normally migrate. Most of the surviving eagles from Norway have remained in Scotland and a number have now successfully paired up and started to breed themselves.

By 1918 the White-Tailed Sea Eagle was extinct in Scotland.

Sadly, but out of necessity, the project to re-introduce sea eagles is shrouded in secrecy because these birds are still vulnerable to disturbance from egg collectors. After much consultation with the Sea Eagle Project Team, the consensus was that the film could be beneficial to the eagles – with 12 pairs attempting to breed, the reintroduced population was now stable and it seemed like a good time to raise the bird's profile. After months of deliberation we were finally given the go-ahead and the *Operation Survival* team were granted the first-ever licence to film wild sea eagles in Scotland.

Livar Ramvik ice fishing

Our filming began with a trip to Norway where the birds start to breed earlier than they do in Scotland. Sea eagles were once persecuted in Norway, but they never became extinct and the country now has 2,000 pairs of breeding White-tailed Sea Eagles. As ever, the weather obsessed Mark and his assistant, Dylan Walker, as they planned their expedition to the fjords west of Tromso. Even at the beginning of spring temperatures can be as low as minus 20°C – the sort of cold where your skin, if it is left bare, will stick to metal. An impressive amount of equipment was amassed in the office but the highlight of the official BBC safety advice was that special chocolate rations should be provided for those working in 'Adverse Weather Conditions'.

Mark and Dylan were helped by Livar Ramvik, an experienced ice-fisherman. For centuries sea eagles and fishermen have co-existed on the fjords. Livar walked out on to the thick ice near his home and chipped through its surface. Water bubbled through the hole where he sunk a line and he was soon hauling large fish up through the ice hole, gutting and cleaning them on the spot. The sea eagle may have the appearance of a ferocious hunter but this was Mark's first opportunity to observe the bird's true character. The sea eagle is more of an opportunistic scavenger than a cunning predator. As Livar chipped through the ice, the eagles watched from their tree-top perches. Like other ice-fishermen before him, Livar left the heads and remains of his catch on the ice. He was not long gone from the scene when an eagle flew in. Behaving rather like a domestic cat, the eagle's only concession to its image as a serious hunter was a playful pounce on to the very dead fish from a distance of, oh . . . half a metre!

The real cunning can be credited to some of the other scavengers that inhabit the fjords: Magpies, Hooded Crows and Ravens. All these birds loitered with purpose around the eagle as it fed, darting in to steal a fish scrap if the eagle's attention was, even for a second, diverted. As Mark filmed, two Ravens stood together slightly in front of the eagle uttering low guttural croaks. They looked suspicious, like a couple of malingering car thieves. The eagle remained fully preoccupied with its meal as one of the Ravens strode rather nonchalantly towards the eagle's rear end. Swiftly, it bent its head down and gave one of the eagle's tail feathers a sharp tug. It continued to pull on the tail until the eagle became so irritated that it had to turn round. At the same moment the Raven's apparently disinterested companion dived in and stole a chunk of fish from the eagle's meal.

When the ice began to melt, Mark filmed the Norwegian birds as they

The White-tailed Sea Eagle – more of an opportunistic scavenger than a cunning predator

Young Sea Eagles

spiralled up through the sky in perfectly symmetrical pairs. Courtship had begun. Once clear of the trees on the rim of the fjord the birds flew together in parallel before continuing to coil upwards. Most of the birds that Mark filmed here were sub-adults, adolescents practising their courtship skills. These birds were probably too young to breed successfully but as they flipped and rolled together in the air they certainly appeared accomplished. One pair, their tails still mottled brown rather than the pure white of the adults, circled very fast before one eagle flipped on to its back in the air and grabbed at the feet of the bird overhead. With talons locked together the two spun down towards the tree tops, pulling out only at the last minute to resume their perfectly controlled paired flight back up towards the rim of the fjord.

Back on the west coast of Scotland I went out with RSPB conservation staff to try and locate a nest where it would be possible to film without causing unnecessary disturbance to the eagles. This meant trying to second guess which of their many alternative nests a particular pair would use! Sea eagles like to keep their housing options open until the very last minute before laying eggs. Most pairs have a number of nests within their territory: old nests; rebuilt nests and new, semi-built nests. We selected a pair that were busy repairing an old nest in a tree which jutted rather precariously from a grass-covered cliff. These were both older birds with plenty of experience in raising chicks and the conservationists felt that

74

Mark's filming would be unlikely to cause them too much disturbance, although he would have to proceed with great care and be prepared to leave the area if the birds became wary.

The difficulties of filming animals in the wild are recognised by most people, but many of our frustrations are based on the day-to-day logistics of filming. We spend hours listening to weather forecasts. From February until October – our main filming season – weather reports and shipping forecasts form the rhythm of our days, although I'm not convinced that we gain much as the weather in Scotland can be so variable at a local level. We attempt to plan ahead, trying to work out where would be the best part of the country to film breeding, flowering or fledging, and when we should be there. Often, we find we have to drive to the opposite coast at the last minute. This means that it is often difficult, even impossible, to book accommodation in advance. Jenni Collie, our long-suffering Production Assistant, spends much of her time at our base in Aberdeen with piles of B&B guides and ferry timetables. When we are working in remote locations it is often difficult for her to find us somewhere suitable to stay and, of course, everyone has their own idea of the ultimate B&B. However, I think Jenni came close when, by accident, she booked sound recordist Chris Watson a room with a waterbed! Too many steps and stairs are a constant source of consternation as we have to unload all our kit every night for security reasons. Noise can also be a problem in some areas – enthusiastic folk singing until midnight is great when you are on holiday but not if you have to be up at 3 a.m. Jenni must often feel as if she has an impossible task.

The White-tailed Sea Eagle seems to have held a particular fascination for the prehistoric people of Orkney who appear to have adopted them as a kind of totem or mascot animal. In 1958 on the Orkney island of South Ronaldsay farmer Ronald Simison discovered a 5,500-year-old tomb buried beneath one of his fields. On excavation he found that the tomb contained sea eagle bones and skulls that had been placed alongside the remains of the island's human inhabitants. I was very keen to illustrate the cultural history of the sea eagle and so, with cameraman Martin Singleton and his crew, the *Operation Survival* team set out for Orkney.

We decided that Jenni should join us for the trip to Orkney. We had to film sections for a number of *Operation Survival* programmes and secretly the crew maintained that our accommodation might be of a higher standard if Jenni had to stay in it as well! Once we had settled into the Orkney capital of Kirkwall, Martin Singleton, and I drove down to South Ronaldsay to have our first look at the Tomb of the Eagles. The tomb had an incredible atmosphere and feeling of great antiquity but all Martin could say was that the ploy of bringing Jenni with us had failed . . . compared to our hotel rooms the tomb actually seemed rather comfortable!

Over a period of 500 years the remains of more than 300 people had been placed in the tomb. Archaeologists have recently analysed the bones and found that the people came from only five different families. Like other prehistoric tombs, the Tomb of the Eagles contained shells, axes and other

The Tomb of the Eagles

evidence of its inhabitants' daily life but, more significantly to us, it also contained the skulls and bones of 14 White-tailed Sea Eagles. The tomb is built on a spectacular clifftop site and it seems certain that in the days when they were more common sea eagles would have nested nearby. History and its many riddles always holds a great fascination for me; I just have this burning desire to know 'Why?' Why were sea eagles bones placed here with such apparent care? Definite proof is almost impossible to find in cases such as this but evidence from customs which have lingered on into modern times can often provide clues. Even today so-called 'sky burials' take place in countries like India and Tibet. After death, bodies are left out on exposed rocks, allowing kites, vultures and other scavenging birds to strip away the flesh. Only clean, sun-bleached bones remain for eventual burial or entombment. It seems quite likely that such practices once took place on Orkney. Most of the remains are now in national museums but, fortunately, Mr Simison had been able to keep some of the bones in his own farmhouse museum. He agreed that, if we were prepared to complete our filming before the tomb was opened to visitors in the morning, we could return some of the remains to their original burial place in the tomb.

First light saw us trailing across the fields with a wicker picnic basket. All very traditional, except that instead of our lunch it contained two ancient skulls wrapped in check tea towels! The tomb is some way from the nearest electricity supply so we had hired a generator to power our lights. Setting up the equipment can take some time; it's often a bit like *Blue Peter*: achieving an authentic effect on screen involves lots of sticky tape and tin foil! But once the lights were positioned to shine down through the small skylight in the top of the tomb and the skulls had been rested in nooks and on shelves of rock it all looked very impressive. The tomb is entered via a low tunnel which you have to crawl through, although Mr Simison provides something that looks like a skateboard so that the less mobile can roll in, lying flat on their tummies. We all crawled inside and the generator was powered up. Martin started filming the skulls in complete silence as everyone soaked up the atmosphere of the tomb. Suddenly, there was a strange scraping sound and a crash! Jenni let out a scream that seemed capable of waking even the prehistoric dead. It was difficult to say who was most shocked – I think we all half expected to turn and see that the sea eagle bones had reconstituted themselves into a fully feathered bird. Only Martin and the prehistoric skulls remained unmoved; he just kept filming as they sat on their ledges and grinned. The heat from the lights had melted the tape which had been holding the tin foil in place, causing it to crash down on to the skulls and flood the tomb interior with a brilliant white light, but the sequence was nonetheless very effective, especially after Chris Watson had added some echoing sea eagle cries to the pictures. It's just a pity we didn't record Jenni's scream for extra effect!

Nothing feels more joyous than early spring on the west coast. Secret oak woodlands are full of Bluebells and a myriad of ferns uncurl amongst the rocks. Having been granted a licence to film and obtaining the

landowners' permission, we began our daily watch on the eagles. Their pale, almost white, heads confirmed that both the male and female were older birds – younger sea eagles are a much darker, more uniform, brown. Researchers believe that these birds were among the first to be released on Rum. Some years ago they moved away from the island and established a territory on the coast. They have been in the area for ten years and have already successfully reared 11 chicks. Since my earlier visit the female had laid two eggs and, as she was now incubating them, she made only rare excursions away from the nest.

The only way to plan how best to film birds is to spend many hours watching them. They can obviously travel a great distance very rapidly and it is essential that Mark is in the right place at the right time. While the female sat on the eggs Mark was keen to film the male hunting. Although the sea eagle may have the hunger of a ferocious hunter, in fact, it is more closely related to the vultures of Africa than to true eagles such as the better known Golden Eagle. The sea eagle is also what is known as a 'kleptoparasite'. This means that if it can't scavenge it will try and steal an easy meal rather than hunt.

Mark had already been filming a number of Otters that patrolled the coastline close to the eagles' nest. With the right tide and good sea conditions Otters seem to be extremely successful at fishing. We watched them as they slithered off the rocks, and rooted around under the yellow seaweed. Each time they re-emerged with an Eel or Butterfish in their mouths. Otters may have a cute and cuddly image but it is not attractive

The Sea Eagle is always ready to steal an easy meal

to watch them dine: they clasp their prey firmly between their front webbed feet as they chew, stripping an Eel from its spine much as we would clean corn from a cob. They have formidable canine teeth and to Chris Watson's delight the loud scrunching of fish bone can be heard at some distance.

It soon became clear that we weren't the only ones to have noticed how efficient the Otters were at fishing. One morning an adult sea eagle glided across the shore to land on a rocky outcrop nearby. A closer look at the bird through the camera lens revealed that this eagle was poised for some sort of action. It hadn't allowed its wings to settle back down into their normal position and the bird's head turned slowly from side to side. Its eyes seemed exceptionally watchful and all-seeing. The Otter fished, apparently unperturbed by the eagle's presence. Once successful, it hauled itself up onto a low rock to eat. In an instant the eagle took off, flying low. Three slow powerful wing beats and the bird was above the feeding Otter. Slowly, lowering its long feathered legs the massive eagle stalled in the air and struck the Otter on the back. Whether it was knocked into the water or sensibly left the rock of its own accord is difficult to judge but the Otter watched from the sea as the sea eagle finished its fish.

Mark was astounded, we had both read of such instances but to be able to observe the event was a real privilege. We both presumed that this was a one-off demonstration of the sea eagle as opportunist. We were wrong. With the female sea eagle safely on her eggs we left Steve Hardy, an experienced naturalist with a passion for eagles, to watch the birds. While we were away Steve continued to see interaction taking place between the sea eagles and Otters, even in the water the eagles would repeatedly dive bomb the Otters in an attempt to make them drop their prey.

By late June the season in Norway was well advanced and the young eagles would soon be ready to leave the nest. Greg Mudge and Roy Dennis from SNH visited Norway to collect six eagle chicks for release in Scotland. Since the project to reintroduce the sea eagle began, the Royal Air Force at Kinloss have helped the project by flying the birds from Bodo in Norway directly to their base on the Moray Firth. From Kinloss the eaglets are driven to a secret release site in the north of Scotland. The whole transfer operation takes just 24 hours. Like all animals arriving in the UK, the birds then have to be quarantined. The whole release procedure has been modified since the early days of the project and the birds are no longer released on the isle of Rum. On the island the birds had contact with the people who cared for them during their quarantine, now human contact is kept to an absolute minimum as it is believed to be better for the young eagles to be wary of humans. During their brief period of captivity they are fed via hatches in the back of the large cages where they are kept. Just before the birds are released they are checked over by a vet and light plastic tags are attached to their wings so that each eagle can be easily identified in the wild, even from a distance.

Operation Survival filmed the six young birds' rather prestigious arrival in Scotland by RAF Nimrod and we were keen to record them savouring their first taste of freedom five weeks later. The problem was that Mark

The RAF fly Sea Eagle chicks from Norway to Scotland

Sea Eagle on nest – most pairs have a number of nests within their territory and seem to leave it to the last minute to decide which one they will use each year

Young Sea Eagle with wing tag

needed to film the birds without them seeing him. At 2 a.m. on the day of release Mark put up one of his small canvas hides beside the eagles' cage . . . and waited. The cage door had been left open the previous night but no one could predict when, or if, the eagles would venture out into the wider world. It was one of the hottest days in a scorching summer but Mark couldn't take off even a layer of his clothing inside the stifling hide. To those familiar with warm weather and Scottish woodlands Mark's dilemma will be obvious. The still air was thick with midges and he had to wear a balaclava and midge net for protection. By first light one eagle had dared to look outside, twisting its head this way and that. Everything needed to be carefully checked out, even freedom. As the heat increased and the air became more midge than oxygen filled, Mark filmed the young bird as it vigorously exercised its wings, bouncing up and down on the edge of the platform. It waited until long after dark to fly by which time Mark was unable to film, but he had recorded a few precious moments in the life of this eagle. Mark finally packed up and left his hide at 11.30 p.m. He had been inside the canvas box for 21 hours and despite his layers of clothing he was covered in midge bites. When the laboratory processed the film and returned it to us they sent us a note saying that in some places there seemed to be something wrong with the focus on the film. When we examined the pictures we realised what that problem was . . . there had been so many midges in the air between the camera lens and the bird that it made the picture look out of focus!

Reintroducing an animal that has become extinct clearly involves a great deal of both effort and expense. Some people might suggest that it would be better to direct all effort towards preserving what we have left rather than expensive reintroduction programmes. Roger Broad of the RSPB has been involved with the project since the early days and he fervently disagrees.

> The point of bringing sea eagles back is that it was man who removed them. We believe the habitat in Scotland is completely suitable for them, attitudes have changed in the interim and there is absolutely no reason why sea eagles shouldn't become part of Scotland's bird world again. In fact, in global terms there's very good reason why we should be spreading sea eagles much more widely: they are under serious threat in much of their range, despite a healthy population in Norway.

It's impossible to ignore the fact that the chief reason for the sea eagle's extinction in Scotland was the bird's persecution by farmers and landowners. Some farmers are still concerned about having the big birds back on their land. We spoke to one who already has eagles nesting near his west coast farm and so can't be named.

> As a farming landowner I think my feelings are mixed. One has a certain amount of pride and pleasure in having them on the place and obviously they give a lot of pleasure to a lot of people who come to see them. Conversely, as a farmer with sheep, they are not such a good proposition.

Undoubtedly, some eagles do take lambs although, as we witnessed, the sea eagles have particularly lazy hunting habits and they may well be clearing up dead lambs rather than taking them live. The bird's diet is generally varied and on more than one occasion we saw them acting as nature's rubbish collectors, feeding on dead ewes that had washed up on the shoreline. Obviously, one of the main objectives for the Sea Eagle Project must be to convince everyone of the eagle's benefits to the west coast landscape. Roger Broad certainly doesn't feel that the farmers' concerns present an insurmountable problem for the reintroduction scheme.

> Our relationship with the local farmers is very amicable indeed. It's not to say that we see eye to eye perfectly on everything that goes on here. But I think we need to

remember that it's not just the farmers that we need good co-operation with, it's local communities because these birds are very important, both in the agricultural framework of things and also for the future of the local economy. Scotland has two main backbones to its economy: one is agriculture and one is tourism. With the issue of White-tailed Sea Eagles both of them come together. Having sea eagles here is going to attract people to the area and when the birds have become more firmly established we will be able to drop the confidential side of things and a lot more people are going to get excited about seeing these magnificent birds in Scotland.

One inescapable fact is that many farmers on the west coast also let holiday accommodation. Despite their concerns over eagles taking lambs, they are the very people most likely to benefit financially from the birds' return.

Although the nesting locations of sea eagles must for the present remain secret people on the west coast do regularly see the birds, and once seen they are not easily forgotten. Sheila Weir owns and runs a guest-house on the coast. Most of her visitors return year after year: they are hooked on the breath-taking scenery and abundant wildlife, including the eagles. She understands the farmers' hesitation but to her the benefits are obvious.

> There's no question that tourism benefits. I'm sure the number of tourists has increased these last few years because of the birdlife. We just can't conceive that people would go out of their way for a holiday just to see one bird but apparently it's a matter of fact.

Sheila is lucky enough to see the eagles on almost a daily basis but she is still very much in awe of their size.

> Oh, it's like an aeroplane flying over – you duck! You do feel the threat and you can imagine just what a wee bird feels like because you tend to put your head down [at this point Sheila cowered low in her chair as if, even then, the big bird was gliding overhead]. That's how they frighten the ducks and anything else that they're after. If something clamps down like that it makes it easier prey. Aye, it's got a terrific presence if it's reasonably close to you.

As Sheila continued to explain, most people on the west coast are enthusiastic about the bird's return.

> Certainly the community values them and are very protective towards them. I mean, right from the word 'go' there was no way they wanted anything to happen to these

birds. We were all taking notes of when they were seen, and if there were strange cars in the area we all noted the numbers because we had been warned of the risk of egg thieves and things like that. Highlanders, west Highlanders, are very protective.

Filming at the Eagles' nest – a trip we couldn't repeat

Only one of the two eggs in the eagle's nest hatched. We were disappointed but it's not an unusual situation. Once the chick was 21 days old everyone deemed it was safe for Mark to resume his filming at the nest, although he did not visit every day. Steve Hardy would accompany him to the hide. After a brief stay Steve would leave, remaining in contact with Mark by radio. When Mark had finished filming for the day, or if he was concerned about the birds in any way, he would call Steve on the radio to come and fetch him. This strange system has evolved because scientists and cameramen think that birds of prey note people going into the hide but they can't really count how many of them there are. It seems that they will notice two people going into the hide but they aren't concerned as long as someone comes out and leaves the area.

In the first weeks the sea eagle chick has none of the adults' magnificence; it's like a rather ugly alien in appearance, bug-eyed, pimply fleshed and covered in pale-grey down rather than feathers. Before it has grown a full set of feathers the adults must keep the youngster well protected from the weather. It is rarely left alone in the nest, one parent remaining to brood it. In cold or wet weather the youngster snuggles

Roger Broad – fixing an identity tag to the chick's wing

under the adult's breast feathers. In long periods of sun it is shaded so that it does not get burned. The chick is also extremely greedy. It has to be. Ten to 12 weeks after it has hatched the eagle must have attained its adult weight and be ready to leave the nest. Both of the adult birds work hard to keep the chick fully fed. Mark filmed them returning to the nest with a various tempting morsels. Not that the chick needed much tempting. After landing at the nest the adult would pick up dainty pieces of the food with its huge bill and tenderly offer them to the chick. The chick would grab greedily at the food swallow it down and then instantly start cheeping for more. In some of Mark's film the chick's crop looks almost as large as the young bird itself because it is so stuffed with food!

Chris Watson was, as ever, excited about recording not just the birds' calls but the sounds they might make to communicate with the tiny chick during feeding and brooding. To keep disturbance to a minimum Chris made only two trips to the nest tree. On his first visit he placed microphones in and around the tree and on the cliff face nearby. From these he ran hundreds of metres of cables away to a gully where he could record the birds without being seen by them. This system was fine for the eagles but it meant that Chris had a lot of cable out on the mountain. On one occasion he was sitting in the gully listening to and recording the birds. Suddenly, the sound from his microphone started to break up. Then it stopped altogether, gently he eased himself up so that he could peer across the cliff towards the nest. Following the line of cable with his binoculars his eyes came to rest on the cause of the breakdown . . . a sheep! As he watched, it continued to munch straight through the prime BBC microphone cable! Fortunately, it had selected a length of cable not far away from the gully and Chris was able to replace the damaged link without disturbing the eagles.

The Sea Eagle Project team are keen to monitor the progress of all the chicks that hatch each year. When a sea eagle chick is about seven weeks old a team from the RSPB will visit the nest to check it over and attach plastic tags to its wings so that it can be easily identified once it has left the nest. Any information that can be gained about the birds' progress is invaluable as it gives the scientists a far better idea of how far the birds move from the area of their birth, when they pair up and how long they live. Mark, Chris and I were extremely excited when it was agreed that we could accompany the team on their next visit to the pair we had been filming. All we needed was good weather.

Rain is a fact of west coast life; lots of rain. Everything just has to get used to it. Water drips off ferns and rushes out of roadside gullies. Raindrops hammer on tin roofs and create instant waterfalls on the hills. Sheep stare blankly and continue chewing as the drizzle clings to their wool and drips off their horns. Even the eagles just sit tight. Elsewhere in Britain people cried out for water during one of the most severe droughts this century, while we on the west coast had plenty of it! We could not risk approaching the nest to check the eagle chick unless the rain stopped. By the time it is seven weeks old the young eagle has grown most of its feathers but it still needs protection from the worst of the elements. If we drove the adult away from the nest and the youngster became too wet it might never recover. We sat in our rented farmhouse with the RSPB team and waited for a break in the weather. We cooked and planned the wing-tagging trip, played Ludo and planned the trip, talked and planned the trip. For eight days we did little other than plan. In frustration Mark and Chris went out to film and record a rain sequence; it seemed appropriate. Mark went to his hide and filmed the adult brooding the chick, raindrops running off its back as it shielded the young eagle. At one point as he filmed the adult shook its head, droplets of rain flying in every direction. Chris was recording at the same time. What he heard was a sea eagle sneezing – probably another first in the sound-recording world.

We had one last day to approach the nest. When we woke the sky was clear and although more rain was forecast for later we set off for the long walk to the nest. Mark in particular had spent so many hours watching the nest from a distance that it was a shock to discover how difficult the terrain around it was. The nest tree jutted out from the cliff at a precarious angle, many of its branches appeared quite rotten, even the one on which the huge nest rested looked of dubious strength.

We approached the nest from the base of the cliff. As we drew near both adults flew up into the air, issuing piercing alarm calls. Chris had already identified that male and female have quite different 'voices': the male's is a high-pitched cry whilst the female has a low choking call. The chick didn't seem alarmed by our approach, it just peered over the edge of the nest. It was probably wondering, as we were, how on earth we were going to climb up to it with all our gear. Mark filmed us as we headed towards the tree. By the time we reached the base, he needed to have quickly climbed up the cliff to be on a level with the nest. None of our days of planning had been wasted. To complete wing tagging, checking of the chick and the filming in the minimum time, everyone needed to know exactly what to do and when. On a cliff face with ledges only a foot wide there was no room for error.

It was Roger Broad's task to climb the tree – a prospect he didn't relish as the nest overhung a sheer drop of 120 feet. He roped himself up and another trained climber took his weight, while David Sexton waited on the ground to receive the chick. While Roger climbed, Mark filmed the young bird as it drew itself up into a defensive posture, its wings hunched like an heraldic vulture, but it remained still as Roger reached out and gingerly caught hold of the bird. Suddenly it seemed more like a rag doll than a fearsome fowl and allowed itself to be eased into a canvas bag. The bird remained calm and quiet in the darkness of the bag as Roger lowered it over the side of the nest and down to the ledge beneath. As David removed the chick from the bag and placed it on the ledge beside him Roger examined the contents of the nest.

> It's only when you get up right here that you realise the full scale of the nest. Clearly it's big enough to support the weight of a man. [As we watched, we all fervently hoped he was right.] There's a good variety of stuff in here today. That's amazing! There's about 18 inches of what looks like Ling [a fish] and there's the remains of a duckling here, probably a Mallard. There's also the remains of another fish, a Lumpsucker, and clearly they've been eating hare and there's some sheep carrion here as well.

The contents of the nest were clearly appetising to a young sea eagle but the smell which wafted out across the cliff face stopped any of us from even thinking about food, despite our gruelling and lengthy trek. It is, nevertheless, important for Roger to check the contents of all the accessible sea eagle nests so that the bird's diet can be monitored closely.

Back on the cliff ledge below the tree we filmed as Roger and David examined the chick, a female. The bird was docile as its beak and feet were measured and a metal ring was placed on its leg. With speed and care Roger and David measured or weighed feathers and limbs, finally affixing the white plastic tags, one to the front edge of each wing. Throughout the entire operation the two adult sea eagles circled over-head, alighting occasionally on a ledge to observe our actions more closely. Roger glanced nervously skywards as a slight drizzle started, but it was only a fleeting dampness and the chick was soon placed back in the bag and hauled safely back to its nest.

We returned to the farmhouse exhausted. To allow the birds to settle properly we had had to leave the area as quickly as possible. Fifteen

Adult White-tailed Sea Eagle

minutes into our walk we turned and looked back, one adult had already returned to the tree and was perched just above the chick. After days of tension the wing-tagging expedition was finally over all we wanted now was a cup of tea and, in Roger's case, a good bath!

We had only been able to carry 20 minutes worth of film with us to cover the whole day's events and for Mark and I the tension always lasts longer than the actual filming. We'd managed to pace the film stock without running out but it would be a fortnight before we would see the pictures when they came back from processing. The negative print is then transferred on to broadcast quality tapes and sent up to our base in Aberdeen. We knew that we would never be able to repeat the exertion of the wing-tagging trip so we were particularly relieved when the pictures came back without any faults.

Although we now had most of the sequences we needed for the programme we wanted to record more of the adults' behaviour when they were away from the nest. Steve Hardy had continued to watch the birds and noticed that one, possibly the male, regularly spent part of his day sitting on a grass-covered hummock near the shore. Early one morning Mark built a new hide close to the hummock. Each day he went into the hide at first light and waited until after dark before leaving. On the first day he sat for 18 hours with no sign of the eagle. On the second day he saw it circling overhead at lunch-time but it didn't land. On the third day it was circling by mid-morning and Mark felt sure it was about to land when he heard footsteps in the grass behind his hide and heard someone softly calling out his name. The farmer, realising the hours Mark was spending in the hide, had decided to bring him a bacon roll for sustenance. Knowing the character of the sea eagle, it's amazing that it didn't decide to muscle in on the free meal!

Later that day the eagle landed and sat on the hummock surveying his territory. A Buzzard watched from a nearby telegraph pole and then took off, flying straight towards the eagle. Although the eagles are generally welcomed by the local community the resident Buzzard clearly felt that there was room for only one scavenger on his patch. The eagle remained grounded as its attacker swooped and dived at its head. The real surprise was the size difference between the two birds. I have always thought of Buzzards as big birds but this scene made it look like a sparrow flying around the head of a goose. Exhausted, the Buzzard gave up and returned to his pole, leaving a rather bemused eagle sitting in the sunshine amid a group of thistles.

However, the scene reminded us of an important issue regarding the reintroduction of the sea eagle. People may welcome the return of the eagles but will the birds be able to adapt to and survive the changing west coast ecosystem? Although much persecuted, the Golden Eagle never became extinct. Instead many retreated to occupy the more remote, coastal sites and eyries once used by sea eagles. Since the extinction of the White-tailed Sea Eagle the Hebridean islands and less accessible parts of the west coast have become the stronghold of the Golden Eagle. Both conservationists and more casual observers wonder how the Goldies will take to the return of their prodigal cousins. While filming in Norway Mark met up with Duncan Halley, a Scottish biologist who is working on the interaction between the two species in that country.

Each morning Duncan skis out to the snow-covered woodlands in front of his log cabin base and distributes carcasses so that he can watch how the two species react. Ever the opportunists, great numbers of sea eagles visit his study site and he regularly sees up to 14 sea eagles jostling over a carcass. The Golden Eagle is by far the smaller of the two eagles but it's clear from his observations which of the two species is the more aggressive.

> Sea eagles are much more convivial birds, they don't mind company and sometimes seem actively to seek it. When they are at a carcass they look just like large Turkeys; they're not really very aggressive or swift eagle-like birds at all. They are far, far more similar to vultures in their general habits and behaviour. The Golden Eagles, on the other hand, will arrive at the carcass almost as if it were live prey; a Goldie will come in very fast and anything that gets in the way had better get out of the way. Golden Eagles are the psychopaths of the bird world, they don't like anyone getting too close to

them. I've seen one male Golden Eagle knock seven sea eagles away from a carcass inside ten seconds.

Duncan's research in Norway clearly illustrates the different characters of these birds but the two species clearly co-existed in Scotland before the sea eagle's extinction. Those working on the re-introduction project certainly see little evidence for concern about the return of the sea eagle, as Roger Broad confirmed.

> Currently, we've got sea eagles nesting within two kilometres of known Golden Eagle nesting sites and as far as we can ascertain the Goldies are not being pushed out. Over the years we've watched the sea eagles slot back in to the west coast environment, in between existing pairs of Golden Eagles which are still producing average numbers of chicks. But we are dealing with very small numbers of sea eagles alongside a large and important population of Golden Eagles and as time goes on and the sea eagle population builds up undoubtedly we will get more information on their relationship.

In early July Mark returned to his hide by the nest. The young chick was now fully feathered and a dark chocolate-brown in colour. It regularly bounced up and down on the edge of the nest, flapping and stretching its wings. A few days later Mark filmed the bird taking one of its first flights. It twisted and tumbled in the air and on some occasions seemed to have difficulty in trying to remain the right way up as it flew but, gradually, over the following few days it became an accomplished flyer.

Before he left the area Mark returned to the hummock down by the sea where he had filmed the Otters and the Buzzard attack. As the sun began to set he filmed a single adult sea eagle calling out against a backdrop of hazy hills. The white sails of a yacht flashed in the sun and the other adult eagle flew in to join its mate. The pair sat, like book ends, silhouetted against one of those very special west coast sunsets and Mark felt sure that these magnificent birds certainly had come back to a future on the west coast of Scotland.

Small is beautiful – the Chequered Skipper Butterfly

CHAPTER FIVE

SMALL IS BEAUTIFUL

Small things are often overlooked, even in the natural world but, as the saying goes, 'small is beautiful' and the butterflies and moths of Scotland are no exception. Exquisitely patterned and often brightly coloured, butterflies are usually thought of as exotic creatures which are more at home in the rainforests of Indonesia than on the moorlands of Scotland. But despite Scotland's northern lattitude and rather unpredictable climate no less than 28 species of butterfly breed here. Butterflies and moths all belong to the same order of insects, the *Lepidoptera*, but there are a number of differences between the two. To the casual observer the distinction lies in the fact that moths tend to fly at night rather than during daylight and when they are at rest their wings lie flat along their bodies rather than upright like a butterfly's, they are also generally duller in colour than butterflies. However, the real difference is in their antennae: butterflies have clubbed antennae while moths tend to have feathered ones or straight antennae with no clubs. So far 497 species of larger moth have been identified in Scotland and there may be many more of the smaller or 'micro-moths' that have yet to be discovered. Six to 12 species of butterfly may be found in the average Scottish garden

Natural history film-makers, especially cameramen, would be among the first to suggest that Scotland is not the ideal country for any creature seeking warmth and long periods of brilliant sunshine. But temperature is not the only factor on which these tiny insects depend for their survival. Surprisingly, these insects can often withstand quite harsh climates but, as their dainty image implies, they can be quite choosy as to where they live. They often require very specific things from their surroundings – they may need a particular plant for food, special vegetation on which to lay their eggs, or the right sort of tree bark in which to camouflage themselves as chrysalises. One thing that Scotland certainly has to offer them is variety, it is a country with a great diversity and range of habitats, and species of butterfly and moth that have become extinct elsewhere in the United Kingdom still thrive here.

Because of their diminutive size butterflies and moths also tend to have a short lifespan and rapid breeding cycle. They are extremely sensitive to their surroundings and are able to adapt to some environmental changes fairly quickly. For scientists, the study of butterflies and moths is quite fascinating as their population sizes often oscillate rapidly in response to changes in the environment. Given the chance to spend an afternoon out of doors studying wildlife most people would opt for the excitement of watching dolphins or trying to catch a glimpse of a Corncrake rather than chasing butterflies. But, as researchers point out, if we ignore butterflies and moths we do so at our own peril for they can act as superb indicators of change, giving us advanced warnings of alterations in the environment.

One of the delights of being a wildlife film-maker in Scotland is that many animals are easily accessible; nature is often, quite literally, on the doorstep, particularly in rural areas. But even in towns and cities butterflies and moths can easily be seen. Many, such as the Peacock or the Small Tortoiseshell are welcome visitors to our gardens, although some other species, such as the Large White, better known as the Cabbage White, are greeted with less enthusiasm.

In 1994 I had produced the first three *Operation Survival* films, but we were scheduled to make a further five half-hour programmes in 1995. Much as I enjoy driving around Scotland I realised that it would be impossible for one producer to film two and a half hours of natural history material in one year and so Jane Watson joined our team as Assistant Producer.

An experienced biologist, Jane was fascinated by insects and felt that there was much to be learned from the butterfly world – she was sure that the wildlife of the cabbage patch could be every bit as exciting for a television audience as the behaviour of big game on the African Plains. Her initial research showed that even the unloved Cabbage White, plague of gardeners, might prove interesting to film at close quarters. To reveal the lesser-known miracles of butterfly biology, Jane decided to adopt a 'typical' garden and follow a group of Cabbage White butterflies through their annual cycle. All she needed was someone foolhardy enough to allow their garden to become the backdrop for the tale of the Cabbage White.

The public response to Jane's search for a garden was surprisingly enthusiastic. Joan Macrae volunteered her garden in Aberdeen and, since it was not far from the BBC, Jane decided to base her operation there. It was the perfect city garden: lovingly tended, neat, tidy and brimming with colourful flowers. Obviously, many hours of effort had been devoted to keep it in such a magnificent state. As I admired Mrs Macrae's garden and her enthusiasm for the project I hoped for the best . . . her gardener clearly shared some of my own reservations.

To show the world of butterflies and moths in close-up detail, the programme also required a cameraman with specialist skills. Steve Downer is a macro-cameraman who specialises in filming the smaller things of life. He also has remarkable patience. Watching a caterpillar shed its skin is almost as exciting as watching paint dry! The project also involved, like most natural history programme-making, unsociable hours. One of nature's less well-known rules is that any really exciting

behaviour, of special interest to our audience, will happen at night. I doubt that Steve saw much of his landlady during his stay in Aberdeen: he seemed to spend his nights waiting and watching for things to hatch, change colour or shed their skins, and most of his day was spent in the engineers' workshop in BBC Aberdeen. Because of these creatures' size, it is easier to film them in a controlled situation. Placing them in a tank or specially built set doesn't alter their behaviour but it did enable Steve to control the heat and light conditions. A special small-scale cabbage patch with real cabbages was planted on a bench in the workshop in front of Steve's lights and slow-motion camera. BBC Aberdeen is housed in an old building and the engineers' workshop was the only available space for the cabbage patch. When we first asked the engineers, they were more than obliging – it shouldn't be in their way and it would be an interesting project to watch. It turned out to be the hottest summer on record and for two months the workshop was filled with the smell of warm cabbages. I very much doubt that any engineer from BBC Aberdeen will ever eat cabbage again!

Smell is actually one of the most important senses on which butterflies and moths depend. As Steve's film showed, the Cabbage White's antennae act as additional, extra-sensitive nostrils, allowing the butterfly to sniff out dangerous or poisonous chemicals that may have been sprayed by enthusiastic gardeners. It is just one of the Cabbage White's quite amazing array of defence mechanisms. Its eyes are also multi-faceted,

The Peacock Butterfly – we ignore butterflies and moths at our peril

enabling it to detect the slightest movement of any potential attacker. As any gardener will confirm, the Cabbage White is not an easy adversary to eradicate.

Male moths in particular require a good sense of smell. They need to be able to detect the scent of a female moth in the air if they are to breed successfully. All female moths produce a natural scent or pheromone designed to attract mates. Researchers have discovered that each species produces a slightly different scent – if you are female moth it is obviously important that you only attract the right kind of male. Apparently, this is one area where human progress lags behind that of nature. Ladies perfumieres have been inventive but they still haven't, I notice, produced a perfume that only attracts the 'right kind of male'! A good deal of research into moth scents has been carried out on the so-called 'Kentish Glory Moth' which is certainly glorious but is now sadly extinct in Kent. In fact, this rather spectacular day-flying moth is extinct throughout England. At present it only occurs in a few birch woodlands in Scotland. The female Kentish Glory Moth exudes her scent chemicals from a gland in her abdomen. It must be a powerful aphrodisiac as a single female can attract up to a hundred males and an amorous male Kentish Glory Moth is capable of homing in on a scent-producing female from up to a mile away!

Cabbage White Caterpillar invading Mrs Macrae's garden

It is ironic that as well as being cruical to the survival of the Kentish Glory Moth, this powerful scent may also have led to the downfall of the species south of the border. The Victorians were passionate field naturalists and the collection of moths and butterflies became a popular pastime in the nineteenth century. Experienced entomologists, as butterfly collectors called themselves, realised the fatal attraction of the scent of a female Kentish Glory Moth and many used a female in a cage to lure males to their doom.

Such large-scale collecting is now discouraged but freelance entomologist David Barbour still uses the technique for research. Jane and the *Operation Survival* film crew went with David to try and film this *femme fatale* of the moth world in action, but to perform the female needs the air temperature to rise to 120C. That seemed rather optimistic in Scotland in April, and, as camerman Martin Singleton feared, nothing happened. Fortunately, interviewees do perform for the camera at temperatures below 120C and Jane interviewed David talking about the Kentish Glory Moth. But she still needed pictures. The crew were booked on another project the following day but Jane wouldn't give in that easily. Herself a fine camerawoman, she resolved to try and film with the captive female moth the next day.

She headed for a remote birch woodland where David had predicted that male Kentish Glory Moths would be flying. As she drove, she noticed that her hired car had one of those built-in gauges which give you a permanent reminder of the outside temperature. Personally, I've never been entirely convinced of their usefulness but Jane kept one eye nervously on it as she drove. The temperature slowly began to creep up but it had to reach the magic number before the day wore further on and the light became too dim for filming. Jane reached the site and parked.

Kentish Glory Moth – a single female can attract a hundred males

After an hour's wait, the temperature had risen to 119 degrees so Jane, hoping to boost the temperature by that vital final degree, placed the moth's cage on the car bonnet which was still warm. She looked closely at the female moth and saw that a blob of orange liquid had appeared on her abdomen. The pheromone was at last being produced.

Jane hung the cage in a nearby tree and waited – none too hopefully – for the males to appear. After a short time an orange-coloured male flew across the vegetation but Jane had to take her eyes off him for a moment to focus the camera and he disappeared. Then another male flew into view; she kept her eye on this one. As she watched, a Stonechat flew out of a bush and ate the moth. In exasperation Jane grabbed the caged female and drove to another site. It was still warm enough for the female to produce her ravishing scent and a group of males soon flew in to join her.

David Barbour has put the information gleaned from studying Kentish Glory Moths to good use in attempting to control another species.

> The Pine Beauty Moth is a night-flying moth which is native to Scotland. The wing markings of the Pine Beauty give rather a nice form of camouflage. The reddish colour of the wing typically mimics the reddish colour of a pine bud and this is where the moth chooses to sit during the day. As a final touch, the little cream-coloured mark on the wing matches the colour of a resin blotch on a pine bud. The caterpillars feed on the pine needles but they also feed very successfully on Lodgepole Pine which has been introduced to forestry plantations and the Pine Beauty Moth has proved to be a serious pest for economic forestry in Scotland.

In the three serious outbreaks of Pine Beauty Moth infestation in forestry, the tiny caterpillars have stripped the leaves off thousands of trees and several hundred hectares of forestry have been destroyed. After the first outbreak in 1976 large areas of Lodgepole Pine were sprayed to control the pest but this created other environmental worries. To try and predict the numbers of Pine Beauty Moth in an area David Barbour places traps in the forest which contain a synthetic form of the female Pine Beauty Moth's pheromone. Males are drawn to the traps and then killed. By counting the numbers of males caught in the traps, scientists can build up a clear picture of the size of the Pine Beauty Moth population and only spray when they are sure another outbreak is imminent.

By April the female Cabbage White butterfly had laid her first eggs. The orange eggs are grouped in clusters on the underside of cabbage leaves. Steve Downer's close-up filming revealed that each individual egg case is beautifully sculpted, with a small breathing hole at the tip. Within 14 days tiny caterpillars hatch out. From this moment on, eating is all-important to the caterpillars. As many of us know to our cost, a caterpillar is basically a highly efficient eating machine. Their first meal is the highly

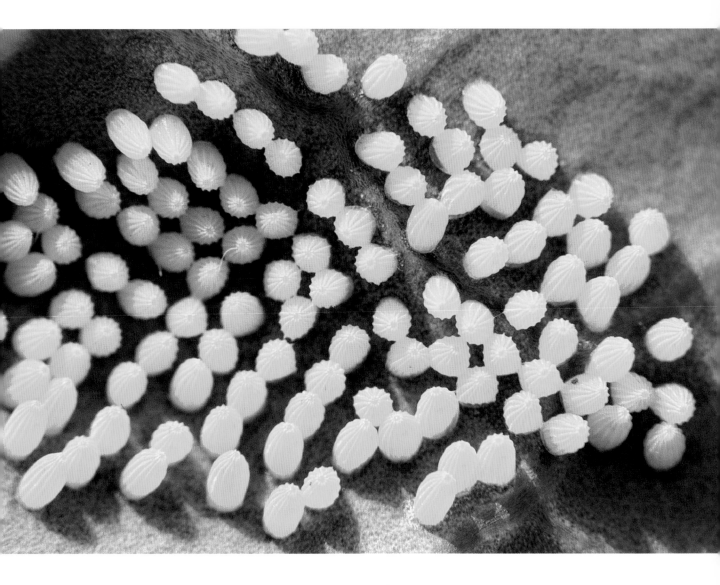

The eggs of the Cabbage White Butterfly – each one is beautifully sculpted

nutritious egg case then, as it munches its way through the cabbage leaves, the Cabbage White caterpillar improves its own defence system by accumulating the mustard oils from the plant in its body. Mustard oils are chemically like the Mustard Gas nerve poison which is used in war and the effects on predators such as garden birds are just as damaging. As far as a Robin or Blue Tit is concerned, the Cabbage White caterpillar is just a nasty taste that is definitely best avoided.

The caterpillars have two different sorts of feet: at the front they have claws and at the back suckered feet give them the best grip on shiny leaves. If the going gets particularly slippery they can also spin a sticky thread, like a spider's web, for extra grip. Watching the caterpillars as Steve filmed them, we were all surprised at just how quickly they grow. As their old skins become too tight, they wriggle out of them to reveal a new one which they have grown underneath. Steve's filming provided us all with a rare insight into a world that is normally outside our vision and Chris Watson was quick to ponder the sort of sounds that could accompany the natural history of the cabbage patch. It was another chance for Chris and dubbing editor, John Cook, to produce a unique sound track, including the magnified sounds of caterpillars eating.

Jane's research soon revealed many butterfly enthusiasts and experts in

Northern Brown Argus Butterflies

Scotland – people like Ray Collier of SNH. He has been studying the Chequered Skipper, a butterfly that has a healthy population in Scotland but is now lost from England. The last Chequered Skipper was seen in England in 1976. It is not a tranquil butterfly to watch, they seem to fly like some sort of alien craft, darting around at high speed in a zig-zag fashion. The wings are brown and orange-yellow in a chequered pattern, hence its name, but this butterfly is rarely still long enough for anyone to have a good look. Ray's studies have revealed that Chequered Skippers have very specific requirements – they like sunny, south-facing slopes, but in sheltered spots away from strong winds; they prefer specific nectar-giving plants, preferably blue ones like Bugle and then Bluebell and, once the Bluebells are over, Marsh Thistle. The female needs broad-leaved woodland grasses where she can lay her single eggs and the males like tall vegetation on which they can rest and keep an eye on their territory. Most of their requirements for a suitable habitat can be met in woodland glades, the only problem is that many woodland glades have disappeared in the last century. But it seems that electricity has come to the aid of the vibrant Chequered Skipper – wayleaves need to be cleared beneath power lines for safety reasons and these, too, can provide all the right conditions for the Chequered Skipper. Many of the known sites for colonies of the butterfly are in wayleaves.

Not all butterflies have been as fortunate as the Chequered Skipper in finding new habitats to replace the old ones. The Northern Brown Argus, a small brown butterfly, once frequented sites such as Arthur's Seat in Edinburgh where it fed on Rock Rose. Sadly, the only place in Edinburgh that you can see the Northern Brown Argus nowadays is the Royal Museum of Scotland, where it is pinned to a display tray. The loss of habit is believed to have caused the extinction of the Northern Brown Argus, although it was also heavily collected in the Victorian era. The sale of many butterfly species is now illegal and collection is discouraged, but Dr Mark Shaw of the Royal Museum admits that existing old collections do have their value.

> Collections like this are very important because they contain a lot of information about the species. You can see from the labels where the specimen occurred and at what time of year they were collected. Then there is the difference in the way that they look, for instance Scottish Northern Brown Argus have a more pronounced white spot in the middle of their forewings than specimens collected in northern England.

In these days of passionate protests against development and road building, it's tempting to think that we are at the cutting edge of conservation, but perhaps that's what Mr Logan of Stainton thought when he wrote in 1857:

> I have not diminished their numbers, having always a wholesome dread of exterminating the species; but I believe a dealer has. And a host of small boys, who come out of Edinburgh with orange-coloured nets, bottle them up wholesale . . . alive in the same receptacle . . . This is one of the evils attending on boys beginning too early . . . Their object seems to be like that of any sportsman: to obtain as many as they can, no matter in what condition. Unfortunately [the Northern Brown Argus] when at rest is very conspicuous, and becomes easy prey for these little marauders . . . In addition to all this, Government has agreed to construct a carriage-road between Edinburgh and Duddingston, much to my disgust as it will come along the line of the present footpath, and will destroy all the best localities for [the Northern Brown Argus].

The Cabbage White Butterfly,
much hated garden pest

Perhaps there is very little new in the world, even in protests over road-building.

The loss of a species can involve much more than you would at first predict. Many butterflies have dependants, like the parasitic wasps which lay their eggs inside the caterpillars. If its host becomes extinct, so does the wasp. The story of the wasp parasites, or parasitoids, seem to hold a great fascination for Dr Shaw. He explained what happens as he showed Jane a box of northern Brown Argus Caterpillars.

> There's one that's stopped feeding and isn't looking terribly happy, it's in the process of being killed by a parasitoid. The parasitoid is now becoming fully grown and eating the entire inside of the caterpillar; it'll leave just the skin. Inside that it will make its own cocoon and pupate. In due course the adult wasp will hatch straight out of what looks like a mummified caterpillar.

To keep filming the story of the Cabbage White we needed a plentiful supply of caterpillars and cabbages. The team from BBC Scotland's *Beechgrove Garden* programme were supportive of our project but keen to keep our activities well away from their own show garden. However, they did give Jane some cabbages to plant in her garden at home. A few weeks later she brought some caterpillars from these cabbages into the workshop for Steve to film. After listening to Dr Shaw's story, Jane and Steve were fascinated to find that her caterpillars had also been parasitised by a tiny wasp. Steve was able to film the macabre outcome. As the wasp approaches, the caterpillar flicks its body to try and ward off the invader. Occasionally it is unsuccessful in repelling the attacker and the wasp lands on or near the caterpillar and stabs it, penetrating its skin with her egg-laying tube. The caterpillar does not die instantly – initially it must carry on feeding and growing to nourish the aliens growing within its body. Steve kept watch on the caterpillars and a week later the wasp grubs burst out through the skin of the caterpillar. It was a gruesome revelation. They then wove a silky cocoon around the corpse of their dead host and pupated to re-emerge as adult wasps. Chris Watson could have provided a sound track worthy of a horror movie. But we learned from Dr Shaw that even the parasitic wasps may face their own untimely end for they, too, can be parasitised . . . by another wasp.

Caterpillars which escape this fate need to grow out of their final skin and become chrysalis. When this time comes they tend to sneak away from the rest of their siblings to find a safe corner. My own office is some way from the cabbage patch in the engineers' workshop so I was extremely surprised when I opened my handbag one evening to find that a number of caterpillars had made their way during the day through the building and into the dark recesses of my bag. Others had presumably found other quiet corners of the BBC building but I guess the true extent of their travels won't be revealed until the spring when we see how many butter-flies hatch out within the building! The chrysalises are almost impossible

Cabbage White Butterflies mating

Meadow Pipit – keen butterfly hunter

to find as they are carefully camouflaged. In the garden some took on the pale green appearance of the cabbage stalks, while others were found disguised as convincing rose stems complete with thorns. Inside the chrysalis the caterpillar's body breaks down into a kind of chemical soup which is then miraculously reassembled as a butterfly.

Neil Bayfield works for the Institue of Terrestrial Ecology at Banchory. Neil is an enthusiastic entomologist whom Jane filmed running around a mountain grassland on Ben Lawers, energetically swooping his net on to unsuspecting Small Mountain Ringlet Butterflies. It comes as no surprise to learn that Neil is also a Morris dancer – this sort of scientific research requires a certain agility! The Small Mountain Ringlet is dusky brown and orange and found only in mountainous areas of the country. Neil's work on the Small Mountain Ringlet was commissioned by Scottish Natural Heritage who wanted to discover what future the butterfly might have in Scotland.

On the day that the *Operation Survival* crew joined Neil, the Mountain Ringlets were displaying. As Neil chased after a butterfly, it landed briefly to bask in the sun. This particular species is like a powerhouse: the sun's energy is soon absorbed through its dark wings and once recharged it quickly takes off again. Neil has recorded that they only ever need to bask for 15 seconds to become fully charged for flight. In effect, Neil spends his time as a sort of butterfly private detective.

> We follow individuals around to see what they feed on but they are extraordinarily difficult to see except when they are displaying like this. You try to catch them with a net but, if you miss, they just divebomb into the vegetation. They just completely disappear – even though you saw where they went in, you can't find them.

But Neil isn't the only one on the trail of the Mountain Ringlet. Meadow Pipits are also quite keen on finding them and after a long while spent trailing a particular butterfly Neil's records often end with 'eaten by Meadow Pipit'. If he gets to catch a butterfly before the pipits, he carefully marks its wings with coloured dots before releasing it again. This process doesn't harm the butterfly but it does allow researchers to track the movements of individuals and monitor their behaviour.

Poised for action, Neil soon dived out again.

> There's one. It's landed on a bit of grass, sometimes they land to feed and sometimes they just seem to land anywhere. This one has landed on some Bilberry and when it takes off again I'll catch it . . . Ah, got it. Now this one is a fairly old female, very tatty wings, quite faded, a fresh one will have much stronger colours.

He decided to take this butterfly back to the office for further study and placed it carefully into what he called a 'Ringlet transporter' – to Jane and the crew it looked just like an ordinary plastic bucket. Neil demonstrated that the bucket had some special additions for Ringlet comfort.

> It has some turf in the bottom so that the Ringlets can lay their eggs in it. And to keep the butterflies in peak condition we give them little pieces of apple to feed on, which they seem to appreciate.

Scientists think that the Small Mountain Ringlet may have arrived in Britain before the last mini-Ice Age and it certainly seems to be well adapted to cold conditions. The caterpillars hibernate during winter, buried deep in the grass beneath a blanket of snow which seems to protect them from frost and exposure. Rearing caterpillars from the eggs in captivity will give Neil a better chance to study the behaviour of the species but research already shows that climate may also be a key factor in the distribution of the Small Mountain Ringlet. A study of old records suggests that it can now be found in areas slightly to the north and west of its original range. It could be that, as a mountain species adapted to live in cold conditions, the butterfly is altering its range so that it can still live in cooler conditions in the face of some sort of climate change. If further study proves this to be the case then the behaviour of the Small Mountain Ringlet could be providing us with yet more evidence of global warming.

Away from the mountain snow the Cabbage White Butterfly will spend only four weeks as a chrysalis before it unfurls itself from its protective hardened case. As it emerges, it forces fluid through its veins to pump up its wings. Nature is remarkably thrifty and the waste products from the chrysalis are turned into the tiny scales on the butterfly's wings. Throughout its caterpillar stage the creature ate voraciously in order to grow quickly, now the butterfly needs instant energy. It gets this from feeding on sugar-rich nectar, found deep inside plants, which it sucks in through its long straw-like tongue. With its wings strengthened and energy levels charged, the butterfly is ready for what may be a long distance migration . . . hopefully away from the cabbage patch.

Paul Baker is an amateur butterfly and moth enthusiast working to discover more about insect migration. He works for BP on their Buchan Alpha field oil rigs, some 80 miles offshore in the North Sea. If mainland Scotland seems to be an unlikely location for finding butterflies and moths, then an oil rig in the North Sea must be even more so. Paul's duties include taking regular weather readings for the met office and this work has enabled him to relate weather conditions to insect migration.

> You have to remember that insects migrate in the same way as birds. The insects emerge in warmer climates and have this desire to move north to breed and feed. There have been days in my experience when I have been in the English Channel and seen tens of thousands of white butterflies migrating from the continent to the UK coast. I would describe them as 'confetti on the water'; they always seem to fly very close to the surface of the sea. If there is a light southerly blow and the atmosphere is humid and the sky overcast, it's usually good for flying insects. They like the wind behind them as it gives them a little bit of assistance coming from the continent.

White butterflies are, he explains, fairly easy to see in flight but it is rare to actually observe migration in this way. More usually the creatures are dazzled by the lights and flares of the rigs at night. Paul does an early-morning tour of the rig to see which species have landed. He often finds butterflies clinging to areas of yellow paintwork such as the rails – this may be related to the fact that many insect pollinators are attracted by yellow, one of the most common colours of wild flowers. Initially many of Paul's colleagues regarded his hobby as a little quirky but now they tell him of their own finds. Along with the more common European species he's recorded a Painted Lady from North Africa and a variety of unusual moths. But it is perhaps the spectacular Death's Head Hawk Moth that causes the greatest stir. In the 1930s and '40s this moth was quite

commonly found as a chrysalis in potato fields throughout Scotland; now Paul finds fewer than one a year on the North Sea Rigs, a decline that he attributes to the increased used of pesticides on crops.

Pink Barred Sallow Moth

Whether the researchers are professional or amateur, enthusiasm seems to be the driving force for the discovery and conservation of Scotland's butterflies and moths. Paul Waring is a freelance lepidopterist whose own lively passion for the subject never fails to fire up an interest in those around him. He regularly visits relatives and friends in Kirkcaldy from his base in England and when Jane and the *Operation Survival* crew went to Fife they found that his moth-collecting exploits were causing quite a stir. Usually the sight of a film crew working draws a big crowd but on this occasion the crowd was already there when the crew arrived. As we filmed Paul demonstrated the variety of bizarre techniques that he uses to catch moths for identification. They all seemed to rely on one factor – getting the moths slightly drunk. Paul explained the art of 'wine ropeing' as he walked round the garden draping the trees and bushes with soggy boot laces.

> This is a technique that anyone can use; it's a good starter method. It's really the scent of the wine that the laces have been soaked in that attracts the moths. Then the sugar keeps them there to feed. As they feed, the wine makes them a little drowsy, even drunk, and they are esay to pick up for

105

Silver Y Moth

identification. I always use red wine, the cheapest bottle I can find . . . half a bottle for the moths and the other half to drink!

Sugaring is another method where Paul uses a mixture of Fowlers Black Treacle, mixed with fruit chutney which has gone off and a few drops of amyl acetate – a chemical which gives off the smell of pear drops. It is the same chemical that is produced by rotting fruit and it's this that attracts the moths, although Paul always adds a few drops of alcohol – stale beer or cider – for good measure. This mixture is painted on leaves and branches and once again the insects are collected after they have become intoxicated.

If the neighbours' darkest suspicions haven't already been aroused by these daytime methods of moth catching, then Paul also has some suggestions for after dark.

This is a Skinner Mercury Vapour Light Trap. It is the best single method of trapping moths as it catches the widest range of species in the largest numbers. It's based on a mercury vapour lightbulb which gives out a very bright light and some ultra violet rays. The trap exploits the way in which the insect's eye works. The very bright light dazzles the moth and in this state it sees an imaginary rim of darkness around the bright light. All the time it flies at the light it is trying to get into that dark rim away from the bright light. So it's dazzled by the light not, as people used to think, attracted by it. Sometimes you see them almost diving under the light to try to get to the rim but as the insect moves so does the rim and the moth can never reach its goal. As a result, the moth becomes very disorientated and flies in an erratic manner. We used to think that moths navigated by the moon and that they were mistaking the light for the moon but now we think just the opposite, that they are trying to get away from the source of light.

Paul Waring with his moth trap

Paul explained that the trap works rather like a lobster pot with a small entrance and a holding area. The base of the trap is filled with old egg boxes which provide the moths with plenty of places to hide away from the light and rest.

The next morning the garden was full with people keen to examine the fruits of Paul's labours. Among his catch was a Silver Y Moth, identified by the 'Y' on its closed wings; a Pink Barred Sallow Moth, so named because its caterpillars feed on sallow; and the remarkable Angle Shades, a master of camouflage. A group of children pushed and shoved to compare the moths resting in old jars. Once everything had been identified the moths were released into shady corners of the garden.

The objects of the children's interest that day may have been small but they were also beautiful and the children certainly learnt a great deal about the wildlife of Scotland at first hand, even though they saw only a fraction of the 250 species of moth that can be discovered in a Scottish garden.

CHAPTER SIX

HINDSIGHT

The Scottish Highlands are transformed in winter; the high glens become harsh places filled with a desolate white beauty. Few creatures can survive the deep snows and Arctic temperatures. The Mountain Hare, well camouflaged by its white winter coat, lives on its wits, twitching and starting nervously as it scratches for food beneath the snow. With black and grey feathers puffed up against the cold the Hooded Crow feeds on the misfortune of others, its head buried deep in the carcass of an animal that had already succumbed to the weather. Only the Red Deer stand statue-like in the face of the blizzard.

Such scenes are spectacular but few of us would want to venture into the biting cold to see for ourselves how cruel winter can be. For producer Jane Watson and cameraman Mark Smith a film about the Red Deer of Scotland was to prove to be one of the greatest challenges in their work for *Operation Survival* – perhaps Jane should never have admitted that she rather enjoys experiencing 'extremes' of climate. In early February Jane and Mark set out for Glen Affric to film the winter trials of Britain's largest land mammal, the Red Deer.

In summer the drive up to Glen Affric on the single-track road from Drumnadrochit on the north side of Loch Ness is time-consuming. In winter the route is often impassable and Jane and Mark decided that the only way to remain close to the deer was to stay in the Glen, and spend the week living in a camper van. It snowed heavily the entire time and the temperature dropped to minus 7°C. Mark had experienced conditions of extreme cold when filming sea eagles in Norway but at least there he had been able to return to a warm base. Conditions in the camper van were not comfortable. On the first evening the team discovered that their baked beans (a staple food for film crews when self-catering) had frozen in the can. Things didn't improve during the week. Both Jane and Mark wear contact lenses and each morning they woke to find their lenses frozen solid in their solution!

Finally, there was a break in the blizzard and Mark climbed high up the side of the Glen to one of his favourite viewpoints, where he filmed a breathtaking view – a still landscape of ice blue mountains and white

Stalker Ronnie Buchan feeding stags

valleys overhung by a dark sky that predicted further snowfall. Winter here is not a season defined by calendar months; it lasts as long as the snow continues to fall. Red Deer have lived in Scotland since the last ice age and with their thick coats of dense hair they are well adapted to survive the severe weather. As they move across the icy slopes searching for the occasional green shoot beneath the snow, their cloven hooves gripping the slippery inclines, these huge beasts appear to defy gravity.

Glen Affric is a natural amphitheatre. As Mark continued to film the storm began with thunder rattling around the bowl of the Glen. Bolts of lightening shot to the ground making the Mountain Hares twitch even more as they scuttled for cover. With the first clap of thunder the deer ran, but as the blizzard intensified Mark filmed a small group of stags sheltering as best they could behind the knoll of a hill. Slowly they turned their heads towards Mark and watched him with unblinking eyes until, as the snow fell more heavily, they disappeared from view.

Watching the scene back at base I shivered – not just because Mark had captured on film the sort of cold that I hoped never to experience but because I realised that these majestic animals are also at the centre of a political storm which rages over the future of the Scottish landscape. Red Deer are native to Scotland but, for the last two hundred years, the land has been managed almost solely for their benefit. Originally, the deer were forest animals (as they still are in much of northern Europe) but as the forests were cleared deer numbers began to decline, reaching an all time low in the late 1700s. Driven out on to the open hills, the deer were hunted and were forced to compete for food with large numbers of sheep. But the Red Deer soon adapted to the harsher environment and by the late eighteenth century sheep farming was in decline and deer stalking had become a lucrative source of income for the large sporting estates. Areas of open hill known as 'deer forests' were managed specifically for Red Deer and their numbers began to increase again. In the last 40 years Scotland's Red Deer population has trebled.

Since the Victorian era the Red Deer stag has been perceived as the 'Monarch of the Glen', synonymous with virile power and strength, but many stags are not as wild as they seem. On the lower slopes of Glen Affric Mark and Jane met up with Ronnie Buchan, stalker for one of the Glen's sporting estates. Ronnie called to the stags as he dispensed fodder from the back of his Argocat all-terrain vehicle. The stags came running as they heard him, behaving more like tame pets than macho stags.

> The main reason we feed the deer is really to keep them here on the estate; to stop them moving out on to the roadsides or falling prey to poachers. The other reason is to maintain the quality of the deer throughout the winter. After a long hard rut they are sometimes in a pretty bad condition.

Feeding the deer also gives Ronnie a chance to check the animals over at close quarters and decide which ones should be targeted next season.

Here, staggy, staggy! Over here we've got two or three young

stags. They're only four or five years old and already they've got 11 or 12 points on their antlers, so they are really good stags. They'll probably be quite big when they get older. Over here we've got two switch-top stags – they've only got six points and the tops of their antlers are pointed. Those are basically what we call cull stags: they're shootable. We tend to leave all the fellows with the big heads as breeding deer and we shoot all the weak ones: the rubbish ones with bad heads. Controlling deer and conservation are the same thing, it's what a stalker does. It keeps the numbers down, shooting the stag's that are weak and in poor condition.

Only the stags tend to come down into the Glen for food – at this time of year the more hardy hinds run in their own herds, living on the higher slopes quite separately from the stags. As Ronnie fed the stags, the sharp tapping sound of nails being hammered into posts echoed across the

Red Deer – perhaps they have been too successful at survival

The Mountain Hare lives on its wits

water. Sandy Walker of the Forestry Commission was busy erecting deer fences on the other side of the glen. One man's valuable resource is, it would appear, another's pest. Sandy Walker doesn't view the work of the stalking estates as conservation.

> Red Deer numbers have risen to 300, 000 over the last 150 years mainly because of the sporting interest of the estates who want high numbers of stags so they can take people out to stalk and to shoot the deer as a source of income.

Sandy went on to explain the threat that such high numbers of deer pose:

> Glen Affric is a very special place because it contains one of the largest remnants of the old pine forest. These are the descendants of trees which colonised the country (most of the country) after the last ice-age. The deer congregate here in high numbers for shelter and food, particularly in winter time and unfortunately they graze on the young tree seedlings which never get a chance to grow into mature trees.

Taking a break from his fencing, Sandy walked across the heather and knelt down beside what appeared to be a Bonsai Pine.

112

Here we have a small seedling and, believe it or not, it could be 25 to 30 years old. But instead of being 30 feet tall and producing seed for another generation of trees, it's only six inches high because it has been repeatedly grazed back by the deer.

He returned to his fence – a substantial structure over eight feet high: a fence that any prison would be proud of.

Nobody really likes the fences because they are not nice to look at. They form an unnatural barrier in the woodland and they are very expensive to erect – up to five pounds a metre. But the deer also need the forest for their survival. They are basically still woodland animals and they need the woodland for shelter in wintertime. Unless we erect fences to keep deer out they will ultimately die out, too.

Apart from erecting deer fences the Forestry Commission also cull some animals. Each group of deer is carefully studied to select which animals need to be shot by forestry rangers. The whole procedure is carried out according to many of the rules of traditional stalking but the killing is not done for profit, although the carcasses are sold on to game dealers.

Red Deer stags shed their antlers in early spring, the dominant stags being the first to cast off their magnificent crowns. Having lost their obvious badges of office, the naked-looking beasts have to resort to a more subtle way of establishing rank within the herd. Mark followed a group of young stags and filmed a bizarre display. About 20 animals stood like uncomfortable adolescents around a Scots Pine-topped hill; they seemed to be trying to avoid each other's gaze, as if even a glance might force some sort of confrontation. Sometimes a meeting was inevitable as the animals ambled around. Once face to face the stags eyed each other cautiously with pale pink tongues lolling from the sides of their mouths. As a mere observer of what appeared to be tongue contests, it was impossible to judge the rightful winners – was it the stag with the longest or pinkest tongue or the animal that dribbled the most? It was easy to see why that great artist of the Highlands, Landseer, excluded this particular piece of deer behaviour from his many portraits of the Monarch of the Glen!

The tongue exhibition clearly does not settle all hierarchical disputes for often the deer follow this with a more spectacular display of strength. The huge animals rear up on their hind legs and paw at each other, their front hooves flailing. You can clearly hear the clicks as the animals' hooves touched.

By mid May spring has a decisive hold on Glen Affric. From his viewpoint on the slopes Mark could hear the eerie calls of Red Throated Divers, elegant long billed waterbirds that return from the sea to the high lochans to nest. The next day he and Jane made a dawn visit to the waterside and filmed what I regard as the most beautiful pictures of the

Operation Survival series. Early-morning mist still clung to the surface of the water and the whole scene was edged by the silhouettes of bent and gnarled pines. At first a single diver pushed out into the water of the lochan, hardly making a ripple as it swam. It was soon joined by another smoothly streamlined slate-grey bird. Red-throated Divers are extremely territorial and the appearance of a third bird prompted the initial pair to display. The birds stretched their necks and twisted around one another in a strange dawn ballet; a dance brought to an abrupt end as one of the pair suddenly splashed forward and disappeared beneath the surface.

To my ear, the divers' calls are not dissimilar to whale song: they have that same plaintive quality, a whimsical sound that Chris just had to record. He wanted to stay in the camper van overnight so that he could put microphones out on the water's edge in the evening and record the birds at first light. We also presumed that he would want to sleep, but no. He spent the night huddled in a quilt wearing his headphones, constantly twiddling with the dials on his recorder as he listened to the divers night-time recital.

Spending time in the field with Chris during the making of *Operation Survival* has taught us all a great deal about sound, one of the most overlooked dimensions of the natural world. At a burn which runs into Loch Affric Mark filmed a Grey Wagtail as it flew back and forth across a stone weir, gathering insects that had been washed out of the snow by the swollen spring torrent. Sound recordists usually vigorously resist any attempt to film in such waterside locations, no matter how scenic, because the water's loudness tends to drown all other sounds. However, Chris pointed out that the shrill 'peep' of the wagtail was still clearly audible. He explained that because wagtails spend most of their lives in this noisy environment their calls have evolved to enable them to communicate with each other above the rush of the water.

The stags splashed their way through the burn in search of better grazing in the forest. The tongue displays and boxing bouts may have established an initial order amongst the deer, but the dominant male continually reminds the others in the herd of his superiority. As the animals moved deeper into the forest the team noticed that he was forever pushing and shoving the other stags around, and rubbing his neck and chin against overhanging branches, thereby staking his ownership of the area by depositing a pungent scent from his glands. However, he would soon regain the more obvious symbol of his rank. During regrowth the antlers are covered with 'velvet', a blood-rich suede-like skin that nourishes the growing horn. The final size and appearance of the antlers in the summer depends not only on the stag's age but also his condition. Good quality food during the spring plays an important part in the growth of a good head of antlers.

The situation in Glen Affric is a microcosm of the deer debate that rages throughout Scotland. During their time in the glen the *Operation Survival* team met with many opinions on what should be done about the problem of increased numbers of deer. Alan Watson, a man with a vision, offered his thoughts to the debate. Founder of the charity 'Trees for Life',

Alan hopes to see much of Scotland forested once again. From his appearance you would imagine him to be a wholesome conservationist, passionate about preserving all life. But even he accepts that there are just too many Red Deer.

Red-throated Diver

> People need to shoot the deer, you know. They need to be culled, their numbers have increased out of all proportion in the last 30 years and more and more deer are being forced into smaller and smaller pockets of forest. We have old trees like this one behind me, perhaps 250 years old and nothing younger than that because of this intensive grazing pressure: it creates a geriatric forest. We have to get the ecosystem back in a natural state of harmony and balance once more. It's in the deer's interest – when the forest is restored we'll have bigger and healthier deer. At present they're not the 'Monarchs of the Glen', they're the 'Runts of the Glen' because they don't have the proper habitat.

Alan attributes part of the deer problem to the fact that all the Red Deer's natural predators such as the bear, Lynx and Wolf have long since become extinct in Scotland, but he is also convinced that economics plays a part in keeping deer numbers artificially high.

115

The Red Deer's last natural predator

The root of the problem, as far as I'm concerned, is our human need to make money out of nature. Basically, there's too many deer at the moment because that is the only way large landowners in the Highlands are able to make any money from their estates. We need to restore the forest without any expectation of a direct economic return from it – although I think there are ways in which local people can benefit from a natural forest, increasing numbers of tourists for example.

When Jane and Mark next caught up with stalker Ronnie Buchan he was repairing a bridge in the forest. Stalking is more than just Ronnie's living; it's his whole way of life.

My father, grandfather, most of my family have been stalkers and whether my son will be or not we'll have to wait and see. The Highland sporting estate way of life is part of Scottish tradition; it should be saved as much as the trees. The fact that some people are willing to pay money to stalk and bring money into the Highlands keeps everyone employed.

But Ronnie is one of a new generation of keepers who fully accept that deer numbers must be kept in control and, to his mind, it is the job of the stalkers to exercise that control.

> Someone's got to control the deer. Man let them get out of control and so really it's man who's going to have to sort them out. Nobody kills the deer because they're bloodthirsty. We kill them because we have to do it for the conservation of the deer and for the land. They're talking about introducing bears and Wolves and what not, partly because they used to be here before and partly because they think it will control the deer population. They might kill off some of the weaker deer but it'll certainly not get rid of the number of deer needed.

Although Wolves have long since departed, Red Deer still tend to behave as though predators lurk behind every tree. In a forest glade a stag sits and chews the cud whilst keeping a wary eye open for a potential attacker. The deer are more vulnerable in the open, so they graze quickly without properly chewing the vegetation. Later they select a more protected spot and regurgitate their food for a more thorough chewing. It's not a pleasant performance.

On hot days the deer are known to cool off in the loch – it was a spectacle that Mark was very keen to capture on film. Once the stags' antlers have regrown, the velvet starts to drop off, leaving the bare horn exposed. Any remnants of velvet hang in itchy-looking tatters. In summer the animals are also plagued by parasitic flies which lay their eggs beneath the deer's skin. Once these parasites hatch they cause terrible irritation and can seriously weaken their unwilling host. As we have often found to our own cost, spending a summer afternoon in the forest can provoke a night of tormented scratching. The water and open hills beyond must seem very enticing to the deer.

'Stags swimming across loch' is the sort of interesting line that tends to get written into our *Operation Survival* scripts when we are researching the programmes but by July Mark was beginning to think that this was one of those scenes that would never actually be filmed. A few days later he and Jane were watching a small group of uncomfortable-looking deer in the forest when the animals suddenly got the urge to ease their irritation in the water. To get the best shots of the animals Mark had always remained well hidden from them; to film them in the loch he would have to break cover and run after them with the camera, hoping that his presence wouldn't deter them from their swim. The water was obviously too inviting for them to be discouraged and, still shaking from excitement and exertion, Mark filmed as they plunged into the water.

Keeping only their heads above the surface, they struck out for a patch of lush reeds on the other side of the loch.

Although the camper van's windows and doors were kept tightly shut, the ever-persistent midges managed to squeeze their way inside and, as they tormented the crew that night, Mark and Jane were tempted to follow the deer into the loch. The team decided that perhaps the freezing winter conditions in the van hadn't been quite so bad after all.

Having remained out on the higher slopes all spring, the hinds move lower down the glen in summer, their white-spotted calves close at heel. As the newborn calves try to master the art of standing on what appear to be overly long legs, the hinds remain watchful. It is in these first hours that their young are most vulnerable. Hooded Crows are quick to arrive on the scene following the birth but if the calf is healthy, they concentrate on clearing up the afterbirth. The hind even licks her calf's rear clean to remove any tell-tale smell of droppings that may lead a predator to her youngster. As Mark was filming a hind, she turned quickly at the first sight of movement in the corner of the field. Mark followed her gaze and captured on film one of those unscripted moments that are often the most memorable. A family of young Stoats had left their den and were on the run. They looked like a group of Disney characters, dashing from rock to rock. Then suddenly they all stopped and raised their heads to scan around in unison. It's difficult to say whether Mark or the hind was the most taken aback by the sight of the comic bunch, even the calf wobbled to a halt and directed a quizzical glance towards the wonders of his strange new world before returning all his concentration to the tricky task of remaining upright and walking forwards. Once the calves have found their feet they stray a little further from their mother each day. The calves then form an active crèche, running and play-fighting with each other.

The scenery of Glen Affric is always spectacular but Mark's fixed viewpoint provided us with a fascinating insight into the changes each season wrought on the landscape. In August, the view along the Glen was dominated by the purple of Heather in full bloom. Even the Mountain Hares seemed less nervous as they stretched lazily in the sun. By early summer their coats have changed from white to brown, helping them to maintain their camouflage year round. I always feel sorry for these hares in years when the snow melts early and their coats are still white. Then you can scan a hillside with binoculars, or even the naked eye, and pick out the plump white dots in the Heather – it must, however, be a pleasing sight to a hungry Golden Eagle.

As the leverets venture out of the burrow for the first time to feed alongside their parents a covey of Red Grouse arrives in the Heather. Soon the Glen will welcome other new arrivals. August is the start of the stalking season and Ronnie Buchan's shooting guests make their annual pilgrimage to the hills.

Mountain Hare

There are certain people who come here because of the tradition involved, and stalking in Scotland is exciting because you have to get out on to the hill and physically stalk the deer, whereas in Europe it's slightly different. There you sit up in a tree, in a high seat or whatever, and wait for the deer to come to you. I like to involve the guests: tell them why we are doing it, where we are going, etc. I mean they are basically doing my job for me. I'm employed to look after the deer, to control, cull, them and take out the weak ones, but if others want to come here on holiday to stalk and inject money into the Highland economy, well, so much the better.

For Ronnie the stalking is always exciting. He seems to thrive on the pleasure of being out on the open hill, pitting his wits against the beasts that have now become his quarry. We needed to film a stalking sequence as part of the programme and Ronnie agreed that Jane, Mark and Chris could join him and a guest for a day on the hill. Paying full respect to tradition, Ronnie wears tweeds for stalking and still uses a white

The Red Deer may be one man's valuable resource but it is another's pest

Highland Pony, or Garron, to bring the dead stag off the hill. Many estates now use the Argocat all-terrain vehicles for this last rite but Ronnie feels that it is undignified to see a stag brought down in this way. The crew met up with Ronnie early in the morning as he harnessed the pony before sending it off with the pony man to wait in the Glen.

On reflection, the *Operation Survival* crew could have done with their own pony man. By late summer the stags are on higher ground and to get above them the team needed to climb over 3,000 feet. Ronnie and his companion raced ahead as the team started up the glen. Of necessity, the crew are fit, but their climbing was slowed by the weight of the filming kit they carried. Ronnie offered to carry the Nagra sound recorder which alone weighs 18lbs. They handed it over with relief and redistributed the rest of the gear. Any hope that carrying the Nagra might slow Ronnie's progress was short lived as he and his guest continued to race up the nearest Munro. After several hours of climbing everyone made it to the top of a bluff from where Ronnie hoped to locate the stags. Exhausted, they surveyed the stunning scene below them – even from the film it looks as though they rested awhile on the top of the world. However, the

120

hardest part of the day's work still lay ahead. A stalker's skill in making a successful and clean kill is in approaching the animals unseen, yet to record the occasion Mark needed to witness all the action.

Ronnie spotted a small group of stags feeding below but getting his guest into a good position for a shot requires real skill.

A stalker's skill is in approaching the animals whilst remaining unseen

> They can smell you from quite distance if you're on the wrong side of the wind, even from a mile or mile and a half away. The wind is the prime factor really; you've got to know where it is and work with it or you're going to get nowhere at all.

As Ronnie whispered hoarse, excited directions to his companion, the two shuffled along the side of a hill on their backsides.

> Aye, a few wee problems. Our stags are down over the top of this knoll to our left, lying on a ledge, but round the corner on the next face over the top of this burn there's another 50 or 60 stags. If we spook those, we are going to spook our deer. But, worse still, over the top of this knoll here we've got three or four young stags just lying down, so we're just going to wait for a little second and see if these deer move out; just survey the situation for a while.

The day had been carefully planned but, as we have often learned, nature rarely follows our scripts, or our timetables. This was such a vital element of the programme that if the day was unsuccessful the team would need to repeat their exertions again the following morning – and they really didn't want to do that! On this occasion luck was with them and when Ronnie took a second look over the knoll he realised that his guest could have a clear shot at a stag with thin switch-top antlers. Ronnie gave direction as his companion took aim and fired. As the shot rang out the other deer scattered and with an ominous 'Caw!' a Hooded Crow flew up. It was a clean kill: the shot had gone straight through the neck and to everyone's relief the stag fell quickly. Mark filmed the scene as the stalkers scrambled down to examine the fallen beast, Ronnie's face was wrung with emotion as he patted the stag, examined its mouth and praised his guest's aim. It was, he said, 'A good one off the hill,' but it was after all an animal that he had come to know well during the winter months. If only the camera could also have been turned on the crew. They, too, were emotional – and very relieved that they would not have to endure the climb again. Now all they had to complete was the eight-mile walk back to Ronnie's home.

It's always hard to 'hide' a camera team and our presence is inevitably somewhat intrusive. On occasions such as the stalking sequence the objectives of cameraman and interviewee can appear to be in conflict. A major part of our work involves building up a relationship and better

Pony man with Garron

understanding with the people who live and work alongside some of Scotland's rarest creatures. This has proved one of the most rewarding parts of our work and we have learnt a great deal from the many friends that we have made during filming. On occasions it has been the knowledge of the participants that has saved the day for us.

During one expedition to Glen Affric, Mark's camera developed a fault. He couldn't risk wasting film yet there was no time for him to come down from the Glen and send his camera to London for repair. Fortunately, one of Ronnie's shooting guests at that time was a German with some degree of technical knowledge, although his English wasn't perfect. The camera was taken to pieces on Ronnie's kitchen table and with halting but loud directions he oversaw the resoldering of a crucial part of the camera's mechanism. It worked and Mark and Jane were once again able to take to the hills.

They were not alone, hill walking and mountaineering have become increasingly popular in recent years. During the stalking season the Glen is also a popular destination for tourists and although Ronnie well understands the desire for people to be out on the hills, it can make the stalking, as he puts it, 'interesting'.

> It's a difficult one, the access problem. There's a lot of people who are very good about it, they phone up and say 'we know you're stalking, where can we go walking?' But there are other people who are unaware of what we do and others who just choose to ignore it. We do have to live with each other so it's helpful if people can be a bit more careful about walking their dogs or coming down a face where there are deer.

There is now general agreement throughout the Highlands that the number of Red Deer must be reduced to maintain a balance in the landscape, but debate continues as to whether traditional stalking and sporting estates should play a part in that reduction. Some groups feel there is no longer room for estates which maintain high deer numbers in order to entertain those who can afford to take part in an exclusive Victorian tradition. But other organisations, such as Scottish Natural Heritage, see the advantages in the continuation of stalking. Jane met up with Dick Balharry from SNH while he was out walking at Creag Meagaidh. He pointed out that the most important thing to remember is that the hills on which the deer roam are shared.

> There's a very important place in Scotland for sports shooting of Red Deer. Sports shooting is not so much about efficiency – what we must use is the interest and the enjoyment that people get out of sports shooting as a way of keeping the animal population down. After all, that's good for employment and for income in the community. At the same time we must ensure that the habitat is in harmony with the number of animals.

Red Deer on the open hill

There has also got to be good access to the land for other people too, because the land taken for one person to stalk in one day is about five thousand acres. The conflict is more to do with the fact that the people who want to walk do not know the reasons why they are being restricted in some situations. Once they know they, too, will want to be responsible.

By October the view down the glen is dominated by the golden colours of autumn, and the eerie calls of the Red-throated Divers are replaced by the deep bellow of rutting stags. The depth and power of his roar is all important to the dominant stag at this time of year as he tries to keep away intruders and defend his harem of hinds. Chris Watson recorded stags roaring early one morning and played it back to me later – it sounded like the bellowing of some huge African beast rather than a sound emanating from the Highlands of Scotland. Autumn also has its

Jane Watson on location

own smell and the scent of decaying Heather and Bracken is mingled with the pungent musky smell of the stags!

The stag has a difficult task in trying to keep his hinds together, for his exclusive use. He is delicate in his affections, however, tenderly licking the ears of resting hinds as he circles the group. To prepare himself for his more lusty moments he urinates in a peat hag, mixes the mud with his antlers and coats himself in the 'rich-smelling' concoction. Apparently, it makes him more appealing to the hinds. The film revealed the whole intricate toilet, including the stag's swaggering walk back to the hinds – it was pure John Wayne! This guy was very sure of his appeal! Shortly after mating, a young stag, possibly a first-year animal, followed the dominant stag's tracks to the peat hag and copied the whole procedure. It was rather like watching an adolescent boy secretly trying on dad's aftershave; he just needed a few years practice to perfect the swagger.

Despite his tender ministerings to the hinds, the stag is a fearsome aggressor: intruders need to beware. During the rut the stag's neck muscles become more powerful and individual animals are capable of amazing feats of strength. Initially, a stag will bellow to warn off intruders but, if that fails to deter the uninvited visitor, he will charge. The pair will circle endlessly, heads bowed and antlers locked; the strongest stags are capable of lifting their opposition clear of the ground with their antlers. Such contests do end in stags being killed and, as he filmed, Mark was glad of the camper-van's protection: it felt more secure than his usual canvas hide.

By the end of the two-week rutting period the stags are exhausted. A successful male may have spread his genes but he will not have slept or eaten for days. However, another round in the Red Deer's bid for survival against the elements of climate, starvation and man has been won. But despite their continuing success in the Highlands a new, more insidious threat, has arrived in the glens. It is a threat that comes from within the deer family and it is one that could push the Red Deer to extinction in Scotland.

In the 1800s, the Sika, a small, pugnacious breed of deer from Japan, was introduced to a number of Scottish Deer Parks. Many of these animals have since escaped and successfully established themselves in the wild. Sika also rut in October and the stags all too readily interbreed with Red Deer hinds. With snub noses and a white gland on the leg, some of the resulting crossbred offspring can be easily identified. The Sika also have a strange but distinctive 'whistle' but it is not always so easy to tell whether a calf is of mixed blood. Although most people are keen to see a great reduction in the Red Deer population, no one would wish to see them replaced with hybrid deer of mixed origins. Indeed, some scientists now fear that there will soon be few pure Red Deer left south of the Great Glen.

Peter Reynolds has been studying Red Deer for SNH and has no doubt as to their importance,

> Red Deer in Scotland are an incredibly important wildlife resource and they are an important aesthetic resource as well. We like seeing Red Deer in Scotland; they are the nearest thing we can get to the African Serengeti experience in the

uplands. It's a wonderful experience, so it's very important that we manage this resource wisely.

The depth and power of his roar is all-important

In recent years almost every aspect of Red Deer biology has been studied to try and work out the optimum Red Deer population. The deer have been culled and counted, their jaws have been analysed and their droppings examined. Peter Reynolds is one of those scientists with the dubious pleasure of having spent many hours crawling around pine forests counting the deer pellets. His work for SNH has highlighted that the key to effective control of deer numbers may lie with the hinds and not the stags.

We know that, because they have smaller mouths, the hinds can feed on much shorter vegetation than the males. As a consequence, where there are large numbers of deer the females come in and grab all the high-quality grub and this forces the males off – they can't feed on the very close-cropped grass so they have to rely on low-quality vegetation. So their productivity declines. It's not good news for your

The answer to the Red Deer problem may well be to cull more hinds

male population. I think traditionally stalkers have been under a lot of pressure to keep the number of deer, especially hinds, high in order to generate the stags that are of sporting value. Now there's a lot of evidence which says that you can actually increase the condition and productivity of the male animals by reducing your female population.

This theory is certainly reflected in the fact that although Scotland's Red Deer have survived the loss of much of their woodland habitat, they are only about one third of the size of European Red Deer and their antlers are far less impressive. The answer would seem to be that it is the hinds and not the stags that need culling, but this has to be done during the winter months. To stalkers such as Ronnie Buchan the prospect is not appealing.

The main disadvantage of hind stalking is that it's a pretty short day: it doesn't get light until nine and it's dark again by three in the afternoon. Obviously, the weather isn't so good; it's pretty foul sometimes during the winter.

To resolve the situation a great deal of compromise is required but after many years of sometimes difficult debate it does at long last seem as though many of the organisations and landowners involved in deer management are coming together and building on the scientists' research to find a sustainable way forward. And it's a way forward that is appreciated by stalkers such as Ronnie.

The deer should be the first item on the list, really. Everyone must work together or something will suffer at the end of the day. It will be difficult and some people will have to bite their tongues but it's got to work that way. They all go hand in hand, you know – the trees, the deer, people coming up to visit their investment while they're in the Highlands. I mean, it must all go hand in hand.

With hindsight it would seem that, whether for sport or as a conservation measure, too much attention has been focused on the Red Deer stag when the real solution to the deer problem may well lie in better control of the hinds.

*West coast woodlands appear to be powdered with a blue dust
and the air is heady with the scent of Wild Hyacinths*

CHAPTER SEVEN

LIVING COLOUR

Scotland's landscapes are often dominated by the vibrant colours of the country's wild flowers. Tiny Heather petals paint vast swathes of hillside a smoky purple and throughout the summer whole vistas glow a golden yellow with flowering Gorse or Whin. Earlier in the year the undergrowth in west coast woodlands appears to be powdered with a blue dust and the air is heady with the scent of Wild Hyacinths (also known as Bluebells). As spring progresses, every field and bank seems to be laced with frothing umbellifers such as Sweet Cicely and Cow Parsley and the machair meadows of the Hebrides are washed with the vivid colours of Buttercup and Ragged Robin.

The audiences of natural history programmes seem to have an insatiable appetite for stories about wild animals, but for some reason that I have never fully understood, films about wild plants are rarely seen. The theory that plants are just not as interesting seems to be denied by the enduring popularity of gardening programmes. If *Operation Survival* was to reflect the true nature of Scotland, then I felt that the series should include a programme about wildflowers. Scotland's flora is tremendously diverse so we were intitially faced with the difficult dilemma of which plants to include in our 30-minute slot. We could have taken an academic approach and restricted the programme to botanical categories such as Alpine plants or coastal flowers but I wanted to represent the colour of the country in bloom; to take a fresh look at the wildflowers that form a brilliant backdrop to our heritage.

In July we were filming in Fife. I spent one lunchbreak lying in a small meadow studying the intensity of colours around me. As I scrutinised the green-veined white of a Butterfly Orchid it occurred to me that it is almost impossible to faithfully recreate such colours in the imagination, let alone in art. Nature works from such a varied palette. However, one of Scotland's best known wildflower artists, Roger Banks, succeeds in picking out the living colours of nature and transferring them to canvas.

> Scotland is its wild flowers. This bit of grassland here has
> about 30 or 40 species – you can see the number of orchids

around in the grass. This is the equivalent of rainforest, except that it is on a smaller scale. The only difference between the Amazon and Fife is that you have to get down to the right level to be able to appreciate it. Instead of having jungle 40 feet tall, we've got it four inches high.

The coastal village of Crail in Fife has been Roger's home for many years. Personal comfort is evidently not a priority to the artist as he lay surrounded by paints on a blanket in a rather wet meadow while we talked. Roger was filling in the detail on his latest canvas but our conversation did little to halt the flow of his neat brushstrokes. Over a thousand species of wildflower grow in Scotland and Roger has painted most of them. His illustrations adorn many field guides and the text books which help others to identify the flowers he treasures.

If I can do a PR job on Scotland's wildflowers I shall consider my life well spent because everyone is trying to conserve our natural heritage but many people don't know exactly what it is they are trying to preserve. It's up to me to paint so that plants are scientifically identifiable and then people can see the variety and riches that we are squandering and throwing away.

As I researched the subjects for this particular programme, I wondered how sound recordist Chris Watson would react. I felt initially that this programme might be a little quiet for him but our conversation with Roger Banks was to prove to me how lively the sound track to a wildflower film could be. On that occasion Phil Croal was our sound recordist. We had all climbed down a steep, wooded slope to reach the meadow where Roger had established his artist's 'camp'. The grass – and Roger – were slightly damp from an earlier rain shower but as we chatted the sun came out. And with the sun came clouds of storm flies. They didn't bother the crew but they were drawn in their hundreds to Roger's hat. As Martin Singleton, the cameraman, filmed Roger talking and painting I glanced up at Phil and saw him wincing. My heart sank as I somehow knew his grimace would soon be followed with the words, 'You'd better cut ! It is a lovely picture but you can't hear a word he's saying because of the wretched flies buzzing'.

We often film scenes of perfect summer idylls. What the audience mustn't be able to detect, however, is that in reality these portraits are often accompanied by the sound of an RAF low-flying training excersise taking place in the next glen, or the howling of a dog in the neighbouring garden, proclaiming to the world how bitter he is to have been left alone for the day. Usually these distracting accompaniments are omitted and replaced with a new 'clean' sound track recorded separately at a time when such distracting sounds are less intrusive. This 'trick' is not possible when filming an interview as we need to record the person's voice at the precise time of filming. The microphone is usually attached to a long pole so that the sound recordist can position it as close to the interviewee's

mouth as possible without appearing in the shot. As is the norm, Phil's microphone is covered with a fluffy windshield – to the uninitiated the whole device looks like a cuddly toy on a stick.

We had already tried flapping and waving to disperse the flies but they persisted with their buzzing just above Roger's head. And all Phil's more technical solutions of filtering and phasing had failed. He just had to resort to some lateral thinking. The microphone cover was sprayed with insect repellant. The cloud of flies thinned a little but a faint buzzing could still be heard above Roger's words as he described the floral secrets that his observations of the plants have revealed.

> The flowers themselves direct my brush. As an artist my whole business is trying to interpret form and these leaves here, for instance, are so complicated that they teach me what is going on in the plant.

From the common daisy to the rarest orchid, all have featured in Roger's work. But his interest in wild flowers extends well beyond his canvases. We returned to his cottage in Crail harbour, a treasure trove of a home stuffed full with the pictures and memorabilia of a man who wishes to remind himself daily of a full life well enjoyed. From a table in the corner

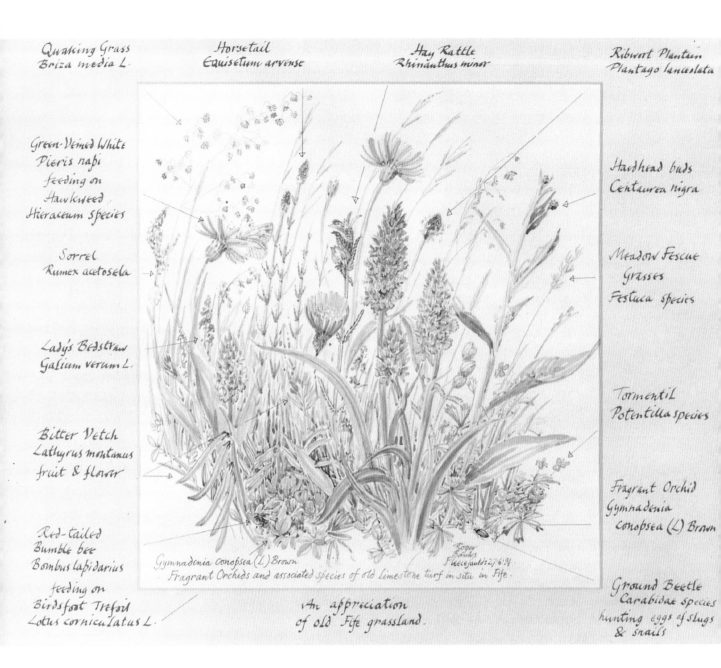

Quaking Grass
Briza media L.

Horsetail
Equisetum arvense

Hay Rattle
Rhinanthus minor

Ribwort Plantain
Plantago lanceolata

Green-Veined White
Pieris napi
feeding on
Hawkweed
Hieraceum species

Hardhead buds
Centaurea nigra

Sorrel
Rumex acetosela

Meadow Fescue
Grasses
Festuca species

Lady's Bedstraw
Galium verum L.

Tormentil
Potentilla species

Bitter Vetch
Lathyrus montanus
fruit & flower

Fragrant Orchid
Gymnadenia
conopsea (L) Brown

Red-tailed
Bumble bee
Bombus lapidarius
feeding on
Birdsfoot Trefoil
Lotus corniculatus L.

Ground Beetle
Carabidae species
hunting eggs of slugs
& snails

Gymnadenia conopsea (L) Brown
— Fragrant Orchids and associated species of old limestone turf in situ in Fife.

Roger
Banks
Fleecefaulds 2/6.94

An appreciation
of old Fife grassland.

'If I can do a PR job on Scotland's wildflowers I shall consider my life well spent' – Roger Banks

of the kitchen Roger continued to expound his wildflower philosphy as he plucked the leaves from a wicker basket full of Sowthistle and Orache that had been gathered from the beach.

> Nowadays our whole heritage of wildflowers is completely undervalued. To me painting and cooking really go together, they are just different forms of appreciating our wild heritage. I'm preparing these wild plants because we have people coming to dinner tonight and together Sowthistle and Orache make a wonderful steamed vegetable that people have appreciated ever since the Iron Age. For me wildflowers are increasingly a way of life: I paint them, I eat them and I'm waiting to be recycled by them myself.

Casual observers have been tempted to believe that plants are rather static and uninteresting life forms but, as we discovered during the making of the film, many flowers exhibit quite bizarre behaviour and plants are always on the move. The Wallflower is one of the earliest recorded invaders of Scotland, the plant grows naturally in the southern Mediterranean but it is believed to have been brought to Britain by soldiers returning from the crusades. Cameraman Gordon Buchanan filmed the dusky red and sunshine-yellow flowers as they straggled up Edinburgh Castle mound, some plants could even be seen clinging tenaciously to the walls of the massive building itself. Wallflower is often found in such locations and has, in fact, become more successful at conquering Scottish castle walls than any human attackers have ever been.

Later in history our own human road and rail networks have often helped plant invaders in their conquest. Oxford Ragwort, a brilliant yellow-flowered, daisy-like plant, was originally a native of Italy. It is a pretty flower and specimens had been taken at an early date to a botanical garden in Oxford from where they escaped 200 years ago. This ragwort flowers prolifically from May to December and can produce 10,000 seeds from a single plant in one flowering season. Once established on the other side of the botanic garden wall the escapees soon spread their seeds and Oxford Ragwort left the city of dreaming spires and began to make its way north. To begin with the plant's progress was slow but with the advent of the railways Oxford Ragwort found a dry, gravelly habitat which ideally suited its growing requirements. It spread with the growth of the rail network and by 1948 Oxford Ragwort had reached Edinburgh station.

Rail tracks and roadsides do offer a relatively undisturbed growing place for many species but there is another benefit to this particular habitat. The air turbulence created by passing trains and traffic sweeps along the seeds and ensures their spread. Many Scottish roads are now bordered in summer by the flower spikes of striking pink Rosebay Willowherb but a century ago it was restricted to woodland glades. The plant only became more common after the Second World War when burnt-out bomb sites provided it with a plentiful source of carbon-rich soil: hence its other name of 'Fireweed'. The name is apt, for not only does the plant thrive on soils with a high ash content but the flowers often remind me of brilliant pink flames licking up from the ground. Never was this image more vivid than one evening when we were filming in Orkney.

One of the real delights of our time spent travelling the country are those unique moments when our work means that we just happen to be in the right place at the right time to witness all the elements of the natural world as they come together for a few brief seconds of startling exhibition. Our afternoon had been spent filming on Orkney mainland and as the sun set we were heading back along the road towards Kirkwall. I couldn't resist stopping at the Ring of Brodgar, a magnificent prehistoric stone circle to which I am always drawn. As I got out of the car the sun's dying rays brushed the flower spikes of a patch of Rosebay Willowherb that grew between me and the stones. It was as if the ground in front of the long fingers of stone had burst into flame. Everything – flower spikes, stones – blazed and inevitably my gaze stretched upwards into the final embers of the sky's evening light. At that moment I wouldn't have been

Comfort doesn't seem to be important to wildflower artist Roger Banks

at all surprised to have seen an almighty hand reach down from the burning sky. In that fleeting second I had gained a far better insight into the long relationship between man and nature in Scotland.

The analogy with fire continues once the long pinkish green seedpods of the Rosebay Willowherb ripen and burst. Thousands of lightweight fibrous seeds are released which billow and curl in the wind like smoke. But before the seeds of any plant are formed the flower must first be pollinated and here, once again, colour and design are central to wild-flower success. Most plants are pollinated by insects as they search for nectar, and bizarre flower shapes seem perfectly formed to entice winged visitors. Steve Downer, the specialist cameraman who filmed some of the close-up sequences for 'Small is Beautiful' was preparing to film insects as they sought the nectar-rich centres of flowers so I needed to find a variety of suitable specimens for him to work with. I spent many evenings searching for flowers along the banks of the River Don near my home in Aberdeen – I always get great enjoyment from such projects as they teach you how to look more closely at the everyday natural things around you. As I walked I saw clumps of exotic yellow Monkey Flower, when I peered into the flower's centre I could easily make out the rows of red dots designed to guide insects into the centre. This plant became even more appealing to my sense of humour when I learned that its Gaelic name is *meilleag an uillt* which translates as 'Blubber Lip of the Stream'! Further along the riverbank blue Forget-me-knot flowers offered a pale, clearly ringed target at their centre, and the pink-and-white striped flowers of Bindweed were bell shaped to funnel the insect vistors towards their core. Although many of the guide markings on flowers are visible to us, recently researchers have discovered that many more unseen lines exist, lines which are quite clear to the insects that follow them for they are marked on the petals in infra red. I am always fascinated by such revela-tions for they show that even when we spend so much time observing nature there is far much more to the natural world than is obvious to the human eye.

Bees are some of the most active pollinators, visiting flower after flower for nectar and collecting the pollen dust in sacs on their legs as they work. Bees will always fly to the most abundant form of nectar and in many areas this is now a new plant invader, Oilseed Rape. In recent years many fields across Scotland have exploded into violent yellow bloom as more and more hectares of farmland have been planted with Oilseed Rape, a relative of Mustard, which is grown for its valuable oil-rich seeds. Usually, the battle is to stop weeds invading crops but with rape the situation has been reversed as this cultivated plant spills out of the fields and on to verges, causing consternation among some bee keepers who fear that rape-dominated nectar will affect their honey.

Giant Hogweed is another unwelcome plant invader. Naturally occur-ring in South-East Asia, it was often planted in Victorian gardens where its huge stems made an impressive display, towering high above the other vegetation. Now its umbrella-like flower heads dominate many riverside areas and swamp the natural vegetation. It's easily seen as the plant grows up to four metres high but it is not so easy to eradicate: the Giant

Hogweed is designed for endurance. Each plant produces around 50,000 flat seeds which are easily transported by rivers and other waterways and many local authorites wage a constant battle against the continued spread of the giant survivor. Their concern is heightened because the chemicals in the plant's sap cause severe burns when those unfortunate enough to brush against its stems are exposed to sunlight.

In midsummer the *Operation Survival* team set out to discover some of Scotland's own hardy plant survivors. We arranged to meet up with botanist Michael Scott and a group of enthusiasts who had travelled from all around Britain to comb the high mountain slopes in search of 'Arctic Alpines', plants which have survived in Scotland since the last Ice Age ten thousand years ago. During cooler periods in Scotland's geological history plants such as Yellow Mountain Saxifrage and Clubmoss would have grown at lower altitudes, but as the climate warmed these plants retreated up the slopes. We met the group at the ski resort of Glen Shee and climbed with them as they explored the ground alongside the ski runs. Arctic Alpines tend to be short, weird-looking plants that look as if they would be more at home growing in a desert. The more severe the terrain became as we climbed the more excited Michael's explanations got.

> You'll notice over there a very obviously bare patch where the snow has lain so late that hardly anything is managing to

Rosebay Willowherb in flaming flower

Club Moss, Alpine survivor

grow. Those bare patches are the places that get my nose twitching because whenever I'm up in the hills and see an area like that almost inevitably there's going to be some really interesting plants growing amongst the rocks and stones.

The group moved slowly, engaging in what Michael describes as 'bottomising'. It wasn't difficult to see why he coined the expression: the group moved with purpose, their noses seemingly pressed to the ground as if they needed to check every inch with a magnifying glass . . . their rears pointing solidly upwards as they worked across the slopes. Michael ducked down to examine a low growing plant with silvery leaves.

It's a plant called Alpine Lady's Mantle, which has these very finely divided leaves and if you turn it over you can actually see the silvery hairs on the underside of it. Plants like this are adapted to grow and flower in a very, very short summer. It's a very severe climate up here, and that's why the plant is here – because the snow is here.

Michael went on to explain that, although there are some environmental concerns about ski developments in some instances, features such as snow fences can actually benefit the alpine flora.

> That snow fencing is here to trap snow so that people can go ski-ing here as late into the year as possible and what that actually does is stretch out the winter and shorten the summer in the area between the fences which makes it suitable for the hardier plants. So, in this particular way at least, the ski-ing is actually helping the more interesting plants by creating a longer snow lie.

Production Assistant Jenni Collie and I had also spent the previous day with the botanists, explaining what our filming of their visit would involve. It's our normal luck to have fabulous weather on such recce days when we don't have a camera but we had spent the day battling up Ben-y-Vrackie in a downpour. A short way from the summit we had been forced to turn back because of the driving rain and low cloud. We had returned with the group to the Kindrogan Field Centre, wet, cold and determined not to be beaten by weather again the following day. On the morning of filming both Jenni and I were well prepared, dressed as if for an assault on Everest. By the time we were halfway up the slopes of Glen Shee we realised that yet again the Scottish weather had the upper hand . . . it was the hottest day of summer!

Seeking out unusual botanical specimens has long been a Scottish passion. For over a century plant hunters from Edinburgh's Royal Botanic Garden have roved the world, pioneering exploration and returning with exotic plant varities, but in recent decades the Victorian enthusiasm for collecting specimens has been replaced by a genuine interest in conservation and many species that thrive in the gardens have now become rare in their own native lands. The Royal Botanic Garden has, in effect, become a plant sanctuary.

In much the same way as natural history television programmes have focused over the years on more exotic wildlife, many conservationists have looked to the developing world for worthy projects. Recently, however, the attention of scientists at the Garden has been drawn to the need for plant conservation closer to home and a new scheme has been started to protect the endangered plants of Scotland.

Sticky Catchfly is just such a plant. It has very bright pink flowers which attract many insects but the plant's name comes from the sticky hairs on the stems which 'catch' flies. Sticky Catchfly once grew on steep hillsides all over Scotland and even thrived in the centre of the capital where it grew on Arthur's Seat. Now it is one of Scotland's rarest flowers. The reasons for its decline are not fully understood but some of the steep, rocky sites it seems to prefer have been lost as a result of quarrying and fires.

Gordon Buchanan filmed the plant for *Operation Survival* just before it finished flowering in a quiet corner of the Botanic Gardens. The pink flowers were already beginning to look rather blousy and overblown and the

Sticky Catchfly

seed pods were starting to ripen. Some weeks later, after its seeds had been collected, we returned to the gardens to film gardener Roland Whiteman sowing some of the most precious seeds in the country. Around him in the greenhouse were pots of Sticky Catchfly seedlings that had already been successfully grown on, but although there is a desperate need for more Sticky Catchfly plants in the wild the plants cannot just be planted out anywhere at random. Their transplantation has to be carefully thought through and involves lots of co-operation with landowners and other conservation bodies such as Plantlife, which is represented in Scotland by Michael Scott.

> Some plants are naturally rare but the real concern is for the Scottish plants that have become rarer because of human activities. The first job is to establish what the problem is for a particular plant and why it has become so rare. Having done that I think it's a matter of everybody getting together to try and solve the problem. It's a job for the conservation bodies but we also need to involve the landowners and the public and between us all try to make sure that the plant can come back to its former glory and become more common once again.

The Sticky Catchfly project is complex and involves different scientists and botanists with a variety of backgrounds and expertise. While the Royal Botanic Garden staff are the experts in ensuring that the seeds are collected and germinated to produce healthy plants, other conservationists seek out suitable sites to reintroduce the plants or supplement the few existing patches of wild Sticky Catchfly. In early autumn we visited an old railway embankment where Michael Scott and Vin Fleming from SNH were overseeing the clearance of undergrowth from a site where a few straggly seed heads of the catchfly showed that it was still surviving in the area. It is often tempting to believe that nature would be best if left completely to its own devices but there has already been centuries of human influence on the environment of Scotland and it is now often difficult to define what is truly 'natural'. Scientists have discovered that the best results for conservation actually involve some degree of 'management' to ensure a balance is achieved between different species. The Sticky Catchfly needs plenty of light to grow and bloom successfully and although this man-made rocky site around the entrance to a railway tunnel offered the catchfly a steep slope on which to grow, the embankment had become overgrown with scrubby woodland and trees such as Sycamore, the area where the catchfly was growing had become too shady for it to thrive. As Vin Fleming from SNH explained, the Sticky Catchfly project is a fine example of how conservation can work in practice.

Roland Whiteman sowing seeds of Sticky Catchfly, some of the most precious seeds in Scotland

> The Sticky Catchfly project is certainly a great example of co-operation between different bodies and individuals. Not only does it involve Plantlife, the Royal Botanic Garden and SNH, but it has sponsorship support from industry. Importantly, it involves the people who own the sites, the general public and the amateur botanists and others who are prepared to give up their free time to work for the positive conservation of one of our rarest and most beautiful plants.

In August the *Operation Survival* crew travelled to Orkney to film, among other things, Scotland's best known rare plant, the Scottish Primrose. It grows on the windswept cliffs of Caithness, Sutherland and Orkney but is not found anywhere else in the world. In making 'Living Colour', we soon discovered that the people who study Scotland's wildflowers are often as fascinating as the plants themselves and the recognised 'expert' on Scottish Primrose was no exception. Elaine Bullard moved to Orkney over 40 years ago and stayed. Elaine is a feisty, spirited lady whose enthusiasm for nature is incredibly infectious, especially when she is talking about the primrose which is very different from the more familiar primrose of hedgerows.

> The Latin name is 'Primula Scotica'. I think perhaps it's a bit of a mistake to have called it the Scottish Primrose because it isn't what people generally imagine as a primrose at all

139

Botanist Elaine Bullard –
"Primula scotica" is as precious as
a jewel would be'

We all drove with Elaine to a clifftop site at Yesnaby and, although she uses a stick to aid her walking, Elaine shot out of the car as soon as we stopped and moved across the heath at a sprightly pace. It didn't take her long to find the tiny purple bloom. Martin Singleton, the *Operation Survival* cameraman on this occasion, peered at the plant in utter disbelief: 'You mean we've come all this way for *that!*' The Scottish Primrose of Martin's imagination had obviously been a larger, more robust specimen and I think we had all expected to see a flower closer in size to the Common Primrose. The Scottish Primrose reaches a maximum height of four centimetres and the bloom itself is only the size of a childs fingernail, but I couldn't help agreeing with Elaine that its diminutive size is what gives Primula scotica its charm.

> It's a tiny little thing and I think if you had a doll's house and you wanted to plant a doll's garden this would be a little tiny polyanthus growing in it. It appeals to people because it is tiny. I think we are all attracted by small things: we cherish them more than big things. It's also typical of these northern coasts and I associate it with the cry of the Curlew, the northern birds and the sound of the sea. To me it's as precious as a jewel would be . . . a little flowering amethyst.

Although it is now restricted to Scotland, fossils of Scottish Primrose show that way back in geological time it once grew in England. At that time the climate was much cooler and, like the Arctic Alpine plants, the Scottish Primrose has retreated to the far north as the climate of Britain has become warmer. Sadly, this means the plant could become a casualty of further global warming: having reached the tops of the northern most cliffs in Scotland it can't either get any higher or further north in latitude in search of a colder maritime habitat.

The Scottish Primrose plant may be small with a limited distribution, but it can provide a spectacular display on the clifftops where it grows, for it is rare to find a solitary Scottish Primrose. The plant is found in colonies made up of thousands of individual plants and when it is in flower the short clifftop vegetation appears to be starred with a constellation of tiny purple flowers. In her years of studying the Scottish Primrose, Elaine has made a number of significant observations about the plant's biology. She works closely with professional scientists, but it's doubtful if funding could ever be found to sponsor a professional for the hours that Elaine has devoted out of sheer enthusiasm.

> I came to Orkney forty-five years ago and in those days there were no professional botanists or naturalists of any kind in Orkney; everything was done by amateurs. It is really rather sad now how more and more things are being left to the professional and amateurs think they've got no place, yet the the person living in the place, studying their own local plants, can often know far more than the specialist and

Scottish Primrose

contribute far more. As we have discovered with Primula scotica, a tremendous amount of work can be done by the amateur studying one particular plant. You could study the daisy in your back garden and you'd find something that the specialist didn't know.

Back at her home near Kirkwall Elaine taps information into a computer database in order to keep her records up to date. Apart from her interest in the Scottish Primrose she is also one of a network of amateur botanists who regularly record the distribution of plant species in their area for the *Atlas of British Flora*. It's only by keeping and updating such basic information that any changes in the way plants grow can be quickly identified and the necessary conservation action can be taken.

From one of the rarest to one of the most conspicious wildflowers in the country: Heather. Heather is as much a part of Scotland's cultural image as Golden Eagles and whisky, but it is far more than a pretty emblem. The tough woody plant with fine evergreen leaves and delicate bell-shaped flowers carpets the Scottish uplands and provides a vital habitat for 33 different species of bird and many mammals. Its tender shoots are the main food of Red Grouse and provide vital sustenance to Red Deer. It

Tiny Heather petals paint hillsides purple

was obviously important to include Heather in our film but we had to catch it in bloom to show its true glory. Filming it in Scotland wouldn't seem to be a difficult task but as the summer wore on all of the cameramen who regularly work for us were put on 'Heather Alert'. Because it had been one of the hottest summers on record we were aware that the flowering period might be short lived, but every time we tried to film a sweep of Heather in full bloom we were thwarted by rain and low cloud.

Although Heather is far from being a threatened plant, the habitat that it dominates has been reduced in recent decades and in many places the purple carpet has become somewhat threadbare. Heather may not be the most nutritious forage plant but it's free and for centuries Heather moorland has been overgrazed and mismanaged. Ten years ago concern over the state of Scotland's Heather moorlands reached such a height that the 'Heather Trust' was formed. It is a rather unusual organistaion in that it has been established to research into and conserve a habitat – conservation organisations usually tend to be more focused on groups of plants or animals.

John Phillips is the Heather Trust's co-ordinator and he joined us in an area of poorly managed moorland to point out the problems. As we walked across the Heather moor, the hills above us bore deep triangular burn scars. The burning of Heather is an ancient and established practice which, if carried out correctly, encourages new growth and rejuvenates the moor but in many places burning has been excessive and the vegetation struggles to recover. At one place John bent down and pointed out a clump of Heather that looked as if it had been pruned hard by a topiary expert.

> The Heather here has been cut like Miss Muffet's Tuffet. There's a lot of die-back with lots of dead shoots.

John crawled around examining the ground and soon found some dry animal droppings which he tossed casually over his shoulder . . . the culprits were clearly incriminated.

> There, you see? A piece of processed Heather that probably went through a deer. There are other droppings here from sheep and there will have been Mountain Hares browsing here as well. This kind of overuse of Heather has caused its decline throughout Scotland.

In some parts of the country 40 per cent of the Heather moorland has already been lost and the Heather Trust is anxious to halt any further decline by advising and educating landowners about better management. However, John Phillips argued that the incentive to preserve this unique habitat is much enhanced by economic incentives for better moorland management.

> All the pious thoughts in the world of how we should manage our Heather are as nothing unless there's an economic value on it. The one thing that puts a value on Heather moorland is grouse because the Red Grouse is a valuable bird when the moor is let for shooting purposes. The value of Heather for Red Deer stalking is much less but if you have well-managed Heather, burnt in many small fires and good control over browsing, then you will have high stocks of Red Grouse.

Heather moorland is a complex biological system and more research is needed to establish the best way to ensure its continued survival, but it is more than a natural ecosystem for in some parts of the country it is also the basis of the local economy. If more Heather moorland is lost then the damage to the culture and communities of Scotland will be significant with the loss of many jobs in stalking and keeping. In such sensitive rural areas the loss of employment also means the loss of the local culture: schools and post offices close and homes are abandoned leaving ghost glens. These are the concerns that drive people like John Phillips.

Breorechan Meadow, the Scottish Wildlife Trust – many corners of Scotland are now being returned to a more natural state

Heather is an important wild plant which covers a large part of this country. It also supports a culture and an economy and the aesthetics of it extend well beyond those two aspects. To me Scotland without Heather is just unthinkable . . . it's like porridge without salt.

To many people Heather is a symbol of Scottish life, it is closely woven into the country's history. It has been used as a building material, for roofing and many early emmigrants claim to have missed being able to turn in for the night on a real Heather mattress. It has also been closely woven more literally, into the nations textiles. Like many other wild flowers, it has for centuries been used as a dye and provided much of the colour base for the world-renowned Lewis and Harris Tweeds. Rosemary Wilkes still practices traditional dyeing techniques at her home in the Borders. I would have expected Heather flowers to produce a purple-pink dye but Rosemary demonstrated that the resulting colour tends to be a warm yellow, although the exact colour of each vat of dye depends on the type of fixative as much as on the dye plant itself.

Looking through the range of dyes from wild flowers in Rosemary's wonderful sample book, I was struck by the abundance of yellow, but perhaps it isn't such a surprise when you consider how many of our wild flowers are yellow. It also made me think back to a comment made by lepidopterist Paul Baker in the Butterfly programme about how all the butterflies seem to be attracted to the yellow paintwork on oil rigs.

Our final assignation with Michael Scott was in Breorechan Meadow. Full of Wood Cranesbill, the meadow is typical of the many small corners of farmland in Scotland that are being returned to a more natural state.

> Wild flowers like this are beautiful in their own right but I think they're even more important because of the colour that they bring to the landscape. I think what we need now is a bit of positive discrimination in favour of plants in order to bring back this very important feature, the living colour of the landscape.

Rosemary Wilkes. Many wildflowers produce a yellow dye.

145

The constant power of the sea

CHAPTER EIGHT

NO MAN'S LAND

Seaside memories tend to be of relaxed and lazy days spent on sunny beaches but although Scotland has more than a thousand kilometres of sandy shoreline, the coast is rarely the tranquil place of childhood dreams. The 12,000 kilometres of cliffs and rocky shores, estuaries and bays that edge the country are ever-changing, dynamic places. The constant power of the sea shapes the coastline, carving out the cliffs and grinding the rocks to sand. To survive in this fierce battleground of the elements the landscape's inhabitants have had to develop special features that enable them to survive in the turbulent conditions. A close-up look at the plants and animals of the shoreline reveals creatures that could star in a science fiction movie. Suckers and tentacles wave from rock crevices, strange tubed feet protrude from anenome-covered shells: this is undoubtedly nature at its most inventive.

The coastal zone promised many interesting opportunities for an *Operation Survival* film. Jane Watson had the challenge of producing the programme, which aimed to show the diversity of coastal habitats and conditions. In the last two years of filming there have been numerous occasions when members of the film crew have wryly pointed out how appropriate the name *Operation Survival* is for our series. They seem to think that the title refers to the filming operation and to how well they survive in the wet and cold conditions! The coastal programme was to be no exception. Jane was determined to reflect the different moods of the sea and everyone knew that none would survive the experience without a thorough soaking.

Filming began with a visit to the Bass Rock, a towering monolith which rises 107 metres out of the waters of the Firth of Forth. The Bass can't really be described as an island, it's too unwelcoming. Unlike the gentle islands of the Hebrides, massive rocks like the Bass and the Isle of May were once the hard plugs of ancient volcanoes, but time has left them exposed as the soft rock around them has been worn away.

Observing the Bass Rock from afar it would seem impossible that a boat could land anywhere against its massive fortress-like walls but the team had arranged to be taken across to a landing stage on the side of the rock from where they could climb the steep steps to film the view from the Bass lighthouse. The trip was in August, a month when we felt that the chance of good weather for the crossing was high. Jane, Mark Smith and Chris Watson arranged to meet up early with boatman Fred Marr, who has been visiting the rock for over 50 years. Although it was a clear day, at first the wind was in the wrong direction to make a successful landing and, as they waited for it to change, Fred regaled them with the rock's history, which is nearly as grim as its appearance suggests.

In the fourteenth century a fortress was built on the rock, surmounting the island's natural fortifications. Welcome visitors were thrown a cable for the first part of the ascent and were hauled up the final stages in a wicker basket. It must have been a bleak outpost and difficult to provision. Soldiers defending it against the English in the 1700s survived on fish brought to the rock by Gannets and kept themselves warm by burning Gannet nests. Later, the building gained a reputation as a formidable prison.

Since 1902 the Bass Light, originally a paraffin-run lighthouse, has helped protect seafarers from the dangers of an impromptu landfall. In the days when the lighthouse was manned, Fred took mail to the keepers. Now the light is automatic, but he and his son, Chris, still visit the rock regularly. Although the Bass may seem unwelcoming to humans it is a mecca for Gannets. It is the oldest known Gannet colony: first records of the birds there date from 1516. In recent years the colony has expanded and thousands of Gannets jostle for space on its ledges. It's so crowded with the birds that it makes an impressive sight, even to regular visitors like Fred.

> It's difficult to appreciate, I suppose, just how impressive it
> is if you've never seen anything like it before. I never tire of
> looking at it anyway.

The rock has the appearance of an overcrowded beach resort but each bird seems to know it's own place. The whole scene seems to be a mass of activity – birds coming and going, others stretching and pointing their sword-like beaks skywards in what appears to be an elaborate ritual. However, as Fred explained, these displays are vital to communicate to other birds in the colony what an individual Gannet is doing.

> There's three distinct postures: there's the sky pointing where
> they put their beak up in the air and turn slowly from foot
> to foot. This is an indication to their mate that they are
> about to take off. The site ownership display is where they
> bow and shake their head with their wings partly spread.
> This denotes a bird's territory; each pair have their own
> distinct territory and if any stranger comes into it there's
> usually a fight. Then there's the mutual fencing which is just
> a greeting between mates when one comes back on to the
> nest – it's just as if they are fencing with their beaks.

Bass Rock boatman, Fred Marr

The Gannet communication system may be elaborate but it isn't always failsafe.

> Occasionally they make a mistake and land in the nextdoor neighbour's territory and then there's usually a punch-up right away. They don't like any intruders, so if a strange Gannet comes in there's usually a scrap. I've seen them start fighting at the top of the rock, tumble down, strike the water and still keep on fighting. They usually have their beaks locked together, each trying to push the other's head under. There's always a lot of interested Gannet spectators flying above them – they like to watch a good old punch-up.

In August many of the chicks were beginning to lose their white fluffy down which is replaced with dark brown feathers for the first year. Mark filmed some semi-fluffy chicks high on a ledge by the lighthouse. In the background you can see the white flicks of adults in the distance as they close their wings and dive like javelins being thrown into the depths. But,

Adult Gannets close their wings and dive like Javelins being thrown into the depths

explained Fred, even at this height the chicks are not always safe from the ravages of the sea. He went on to describe the worst storms he had witnessed in his years on the Bass.

Way back in the winter of 1947 we had a succession of severe gales from the south-east. The top of the Bass light is 150 feet above sea level and the spray from the sea was reaching the very top. A few years back we also had a severe storm in July which washed all the young Gannets out from their nests. The east side of the rock looked like a battlefield, strewn with dead bodies.

Many hundreds of thousands of sea birds occupy the sea cliffs around Scotland and each different species seems to have its own place in what our narrator, Mark Stephen, described as 'an avian high-rise block'. In many sites every ledge seems to be occupied and, where it's safe enough to peer over, you may see the tail of a Kittiwake poking out from behind a tenacious pink tuft of Sea Thrift. Puffins dig cliff top bunkers with their strong paddle feet so that their young may be raised in the protection of a burrow. Neat rows of slate-black Guillemots occupy the upper ledges,

150

while their cousins, the Razorbills, prefer the lower levels, often nesting in the rubble at the base of the cliff. Each species of bird seems to have specially adapted to cope with life on the edge: the Guillemots' eggs are long and thin, designed so that they won't roll off the ledge, while the Fulmars which drift in the wind around the top of the cliffs deter predators from their exposed nests by snorting foul-smelling oil from tubed nostrils.

For centuries people have lived near the coast to take advantage of its abundant riches

Seabirds are now protected by law but for many centuries the people of Scotland have harvested them along with the other riches of the seashore. From the ruins of ancient brochs we can see that many pre-historic people built their homes near the coast, presumably to take advantage of the abundant seafood to be found there.

The plantlife of the coast is also a rich source of food. Nowadays seaweed in Scotland is more likely to be eaten by livestock than people but archaeological evidence suggests that prehistoric people used seaweed to wrap and cook shellfish. St Columba also reflected on the virtues of collecting a seaweed called 'Dulse', traditionally used as a flavouring in mutton and barley soup.

Today Dulse, a purplish-red weed, is a firm favourite with seaweed expert Julian Clokie, whose company picks and prepares a variety of edible weeds, many of which are exported. Jane arranged to meet Julian for some filming at Mallaig, on the west coast. Like so many people with a passionate expertise in something, Julian appeared to be unstoppable once you started talking to him about seaweed. Unfortunately, the filming coincided with the tail end of a hurricane that had ravaged the eastern coast of America and Mallaig was swept by a fierce storm. Jane will not give in easily and for a while the crew persevered, but even Julian's enthusiasm became dampened. Soaking wet, the team retired for the day to a nearby pub. For safety reasons we always ensure that while on location crews keep in regular contact with our Aberdeen base. That day we waited in vain for the expected call from Jane. Listening to the weather reports on the radio, we wondered how on earth Jane and the team were managing. Little did we know that, while the storm-damaged phone lines were down, they had spent a cosy day playing pool!

By the next day the rain had simmered to a drizzle and it was possible to film Julian has he explained the potential of seaweed.

> There are in the region of 2,000 species of seaweed in Scotland, of which 50 to 60 would have some definite commercial use. Sugarware is one of my favourites, it's an excellent sea vegetable, and Dabberlocks is another intriguing species. If you see it in the waves it lies in great long parallel strands that ripple with the movement of the water. Some people have argued that its name means 'mermaid's hair' while others claim that it means 'greasy hair' . . . I prefer mermaid's hair.

The industrial potential of various seaweeds was recognised at an early date and in the seventeenth century the ash produced from burnt kelp

was used in the manufacture of soap and glass. The most important chemical found in seaweed is alginic acid, a versatile substance which is still used to put a shine on paper, to hold the head on beer, for making the metal of dental crowns pliable and rubbery, and as a gel in ice-cream. It's even used to help form the meaty chunks in dog food.

Although Julian exploits seaweed for commercial purposes he is keen to emphasise that it's a resource to be managed with great care.

Julian Clokie harvesting a favourite seaweed

> Being on an island we are surrounded by the most extra-ordinary potential but it is extremely easy to degrade the resource and not to pick it properly. Access to our shores and harvesting of the weeds are always carried out in an environ-mentally friendly way which ensures regrowth.

Beneath the waves the long ribbons of weed are continually tossed by the action of the sea. Slime is secreted on the surface of the tough leathery blades to prevent the weed being torn as it rubs across the rocks. As the flat rocks on the shore are pounded by wave-flung stones and polished by grinding sand, small hollows are formed which trap water when the tides receed. These rock pools are frequented by a range of creatures adapted to survive the turbulent lifestyle.

We considered talking to researchers and marine biologists about the life of rock pools but soon came to the conclusion that the true magic of the pools is best discovered through the eyes of a child. Rebecca, the six-year-old daughter of our narrator, Mark Stephen, was most enthusiastic about a chance to explore, especially when she realised that a day's filming might mean missing school. Despite the thick coastal fog, known on the east coast as 'haar', Rebecca was soon paddling.

As she put her foot in the first pool, a Hermit Crab scuttled across the bottom. These crabs are soft-bodied and use the shells of other animals to provide them with protection – we filmed one as it wriggled into the abandoned shell of a Whelk. Rebecca picked up a Starfish and turned it over to examine the hundreds of tiny sucker feet that it uses to cling on to slippery rocks. Barefooted, she winced as she walked across the rocks, her feet were scuffing on sharp Barnacle shells. Barnacles cement the head end of their shells to the rock surface. Once the water covers them the thick central armour plating of the Barnacle slides back and their feet stick out of the top of the shell to catch passing morsels. Brightly coloured Sea Anemones stretch out tentacles armed with poisoned darts. Conical Limpet shells cling to the rocks. No matter how hard Rebecca tried to prise them away from the home patch they had worn in the rock they wouldn't budge. When the tide comes in they move away from their well-worn patch to graze on the slimy algae.

Many of Scotland's rocky coasts harbour giants as well as smaller sea creatures. The Grey Seal is one of our largest native carnivores, weighing up to 280 kilograms. These seals are not averse to troubled waters for they inhabit the rocky shores of exposed coasts. Lacking the cute chubby features of their cousins, the Common Seals, Grey Seal males have a distinctive 'Roman' nose. Their eyes also appear to be less rounded, giving them a rather wicked appearance as they lean back in the water and stare at you down their long noses.

A third of the world's Grey Seals are to be found in Scotland. The animals spend most of the year at sea but in October they haul out to give birth to their pups and mate. Jane Watson decided that the autumn would be an ideal time to go and meet Paddy Pomeroy from the Sea Mammal Research Unit who is studying the seals that come ashore on the Isle of May.

> We're 25 miles from Edinburgh and we're sitting in the biggest Grey Seal colony on the eastern coast of the UK. It's really quite an incredible place. The Grey Seals that breed here on the Isle of May are capable of moving over a large range. They can travel several hundred miles at a time. We're very interested in looking at what sort of things might have an impact on the population, like interaction with fisheries and potential conflicts with pollutants. The more we can find out about the biology of Grey Seals the better we are able to answer questions about them.

And a lot of questions are being asked about Grey Seals. The animals can dive to depths of over a hundred metres to feed on flatfish and molluscs but they also consume large quantities of the species of fish sought by commercial fishermen. Numbers of Grey Seals have increased steadily in the last 20 years and as an adult seal eats several kilograms of fish a day there is some conflict between seals and the fishing community.

Interest in what is happening to the Grey Seal population means that much of the work on the Isle of May is focused on their breeding habits. Male Grey Seals mate with more than one female and, as Paddy explained, mating here is a violent business.

> Whenever you find two males that are quite closely matched blood will often be shed because the stakes are quite high. This is the opportunity the males have once a year to breed and contribute to the next generation. It's really easy to tell males that are experienced breeders because they develop a rough, scarred neck.

The violence of the males' competitive bouts originally led scientists to think that the most aggressive and dominant males won mating opportunities with more females. However, the researchers' work has revealed that many females seem to accept the same partner every year and it's not neccessarily the best fighters that succeed.

When the pups are first born they are covered with a woolly grey down. Their mothers are extremely protective and frantically beat their flippers on the surface of the water as a warning to other animals not to come too near. During the period that the female is feeding her pup with a thick, rich milk she will lose nearly half her body weight while the pup trebles its own weight.

Chris Watson described the Isle of May as 'the sort of place you wouldn't go back to'. The island has a slightly spooky feeling created, I think, by the abandoned Second World War buildings that are dotted about. Most of the researchers stay in a bunk house in the old radar station. Only the warden has the delights of the wooden building known, for obvious reasons, as 'Mouse House'. Jane, Mark and Chris were to share the researchers' accommodation on a self-catering basis. They set off in high spirits and began by filming the seals.

On the second day the weather changed and in the face of a howling gale they could no longer film or record. The plan was to spend three days with the researchers but five days later I received a relayed telephone message in Aberdeen, explaining that the boatman was still unable to retrieve the team because of rough seas. As they hadn't taken enough food for that length of time, we were beginning to wonder about them but it seems that the researchers took pity on the crew and fed them copious amounts of treacle pudding!

Chris Watson was the most frustrated of the team. The seals were

Grey Seal, giant of the rocky shore

Lion's Mane Jellyfish

making some amazing calls. By around 4 p.m. each day dusk settled on the island and then the siren-like wailing began in the colony. One male seal was known to the researchers as the 'plexi-male' because he made the sort of sound that plexi-glass makes when you wobble it. He always seemed to make the call with his nostrils clamped shut and researchers believe it's possible that this is a call usually made underwater which, for some reason, this animal has started using on the surface. Day after day the sound of the storm drowned out Chris's recordings; he was convinced that as soon as the weather abated he would have to leave the island frustrated. Fortunately, when the wind first dropped the sea still had too much of a swell for the boatman so Chris did manage to record plenty of wailing, puffing and snorting as the giants went about their amours.

Strong autumn gales rip the seaweed from rocks and cast it on to the beach where it begins to decay, providing a home for tiny creatures like Sand Hoppers. Dunlin, wading birds whose black belly feathers make them look as if they have rested on a patch of oil, rarely pause as they pick over the weed in search of Sand Hoppers. Turnstones with their blunt, tipped-up beaks behave like minature bulldozers, pushing and shoving at pebbles to expose the marine invertebrates beneath. Many of Scotland's sandier beaches are combed by Sanderling, small wading birds that race across the sand, pecking with great rapidity as if they are driven by clockwork motors. They are continually probing for the edible morsels left stranded on the tideline.

Beach combing can also be profitable for naturalists. For 17 years Bob Davis was warden of the Scottish Natural Heritage Sands of Forvie Nature Reserve on the Ythan estuary. A whimsical character, tall and lean with a long wispy beard, the coast is obviously Bob's own natural habitat.

> Everytime you come along there's something different – from shells to feathers to bits of seaweed to animals that look like plants and plants that look like animals. The beauty of the beach is that it gives people an idea about what's in the sea. You don't have to get your feet wet if you don' want to and wherever you live in Scotland you're only about a hundred kilometres from the coast.

Rebecca Stephen – the true magic of rock pools is best seen through a child's eyes

As he wandered along the beach towards the camera with his long, long beard literally blowing in the wind, Bob was for ever darting this way and that to snatch at some new treasure.

> That's nice. It's what we call a flotsam hairball. No one really has any idea how it's formed, we can only guess that it is Marram roots that have been pounded and pounded into this really beautiful shape. It's just ideal for a game of beach cricket. I'll hang on to it.

Within a few minutes of pocketing the hairball he had discovered something new to wonder at,

> There's a Lion's Mane Jellyfish, beautiful things. Sometimes they are absolutely massive – oh, I've seen them as big as the top of a coffee table! But if you are a swimmer or a Salmon fisherman they are really dangerous. They have a terrific sting.

He pointed at the lump of translucent jelly on the sand. It didn't look like either a creature of great beauty or a dangerous beast but, as Bob explained, once it was in the water the long stingers would trail out to catch prey and they pack a potent punch to anyone who accidentally brushes them. His next find was a group of jelly-like animals, lying on the sand like peeled grapes.

> Sea Gooseberries, as they're called, form part of the plankton which floats in the sea. Sometimes it fluoresces – we don't really know why, but if there are Salmon nets or something on the beach that trap it the whole mass just shimmers and twinkles; it's really magic.

On most occasions *Operation Survival* has focused on the way that people in Scotland are working to resist the changes to our environment that are caused by human action. But many of the constant alterations to the outline of the coast tend to be caused by natural processes. Wind and waves work together to create the magical forms in rock, sand and mud. The shifting of sands and mobile dunes were explained to Jane by John Smith from the University of Aberdeen, who has been studying the dune systems of the north-east coast.

> Big storms are fairly fundamental in forming dunes. The tide and waves bring in dry sand and this is driven across the beach by the wind and accumulates round obstacles on the beach, such as piles of seaweed or the carcass of a seabird. The sand gradually gathers at the back of the beach by a process known as 'saltation' which operates a bit like the old wartime game of Shove Ha'penny: grains of sand are lifted and carried by the wind and as they are deposited they expose the next grains to the same process.

Once the dunes have been formed they are gradually stabilised by plants such as Marram Grass. Its extensive underground roots help bind the sand and dense rough leaves form a wind barrier. Eventually, grasses, lichens and herbs such as Crowberry take over from the Marram and pasture land is formed. Such land may be marginal but, as John pointed out, it is useful.

> In certain parts of Scotland people still use the dunes for agriculture, particularly in the machair on the west coast. Traditionally, these lands were fertilised by seaweed but in the eighteenth and early nineteenth centuries the seaweed was taken away for industrial purposes. Gradually, the dune soils lost their source of nutrient and in many areas the dunes became eroded.

Past changes in the shape of the coastline have produced dramatic results. The land known as Culbin, on the banks of the Findhorn River, was a productive farming area until the late seventeenth century. Barley, Wheat and Oats all thrived on the rich river soils but the shore beyond the river mouth was covered in tons of sand. During 1694 fierce westerly gales caused great quantities of sand to drift eastwards towards the Culbin estate. In what has been described by later authors as a final sand storm, the fields and houses of the estate were covered.

The battle between the land and sea is eternal: a constantly repeated series of attacks and retreats by the waves. Yet if predictions of global warming are true the retreats may not be so great as the sea level rises. The first places to disappear will be the huge flat expanses of estuarine mud. Estuaries like the Solway act as a kind of service station for many of the migrating birds that pass through Scotland. The *Operation Survival* team drove down to south-west Scotland to meet Chris Rollie from the Royal Society for the Protection of Birds. As they squelched across the estuary, Chris bent down and squeezed oozing mud through his hand in front of the camera.

This is the stuff that makes the Solway famous, as far as the
birds are concerned. Over 120,000 birds come each winter
to rely on the food they find in mud like this. It's teeming
full of life – Bivalves, shells, Lugworms – they all form the
food of a variety of different birds.

The ever-changing coast – Culbin

The spectacle of thousands of wading birds wheeling through the sky is
an amazing sight. They all seem to move together in perfect symmetry,
changing speed and direction in harmony. As one they settle again on the
sand and start racing to and fro just in front of the surf.

The loss of the estuaries and the species that live there because of a sea
level rise would be devastating but Chris Rollie also had some hope for
Scotland.

In fact, global warming is going to have a more serious effect
in England because England is actually slipping downwards

and Scotland is tilting up. It dates back to the Ice Age. The weight of the ice apparently forced Scotland down and ever since the ice melted it's been slowly springing back up. So I think at the moment, and the jury's still out on some of these things, that generally speaking in Scotland the land is rising more quickly than the sea is through global warming.

A great deal more research is still necessary to determine the exact situation with regard to the effects of global warming, but Chris Rollie's optimistic thoughts about the future of Scotland did seem to be a good place to conclude the second series of *Operation Survival*. Leaving the Solway Firth on a bleak autumn afternoon, the team returned to Aberdeen where the editing of the programmes was well under way.

For me, editing is one of the most pleasurable aspects of programme-making. It is a time to reflect. As our films follow the natural history year it is usually late autumn before we can begin the editing. The hours spent alongside an editor in a darkened room full of computers and monitors may be long but the images of wildflower meadows and Bluebell woods provide great sustenance to the spirit on grim, grey mornings. Few people have such a wonderful chance to relive their summer's work in full colour! It must be doubly frustrating for our two editors, Phil Wilkinson and Rob Shortland, who have spent their summers confined to the edit suite, but both have added a great deal to the programmes with their flair and technical experience.

As producers, Jane and I work through all the pictures and interviews and compile a list of shots that will tell the story for each programme. We then sit, huddled over endless mugs of tea alongside Phil or Rob as the film that we have run a thousand times over in our head becomes a reality on the screen. But the exact cut that perfectly captures an animal's movement is usually down to the editor's eye and experience.

The editors are just two of the many people involved in bringing *Operation Survival* successfully to the screen who never experience the breathtaking views or smell autumn moorland. John Cowie, our engineering supervisor, is another key figure behind the scenes who rarely sees the light of day. John grew up in the coastal town of Buckie and has long been enthusiastic about *Operation Survival*. The morning after the programme 'Local Heroes' had been transmitted John told me, 'Last night when I watched the programme . . . I could smell the diesel and the sea.' I knew then that all the team's efforts had paid off. We had managed to recreate a little of the magic of the wild places of Scotland.